The Elements of Mental Tests

The Elements of Mental Tests

Second Edition

John D. Mayer

MOMENTUM PRESS HEALTH

MOMENTUM PRESS, LLC, NEW YORK

The Elements of Mental Tests, Second Edition

First published in 2015 by the author
Durham, NH

ISBN-13: 978-1-60650-759-9 (paperback)
ISBN-13: 978-1-60650-760-5 (e-book)

Momentum Press Psychology Collection

Cover and interior design by Exeter Premedia Services Private Ltd., Chennai, India

First edition: 2015
Second edition: 2016

10 9 8 7 6 5 4 3 2 1

Printed in the United States of America.

Abstract

The Elements of Mental Tests provides an introduction to mental testing and the use of psychological and educational measures. *Part I: The Elements of Measurement* introduces the types of educational and psychological tests commonly in use, the test data those measures collect, and the types of test items that make up a test. *Part II: The Elements of Test Scores* introduces the mathematical models that professionals use to represent test-takers' answers to test questions. *Part II* begins with a review of basic statistics particularly relevant to measurement, including the conversion of test scores to z-scores and the use of correlation coefficients to relate test items and tests to one another. *Part II* continues with an integrated introduction to both Classical Test Theory and Item Response Theory—the most influential methods for understanding tests in use today. *Part III: The Elements of Test Quality*, examines the standards of good testing including a test's reliability and its precision of measurement, the evaluation of test validity, and the features of a good test administration. Altogether, the book provides a comprehensive foundation for readers who are interested in tests, in testing, and in the use of tests in contemporary life.

Keywords

Classical Test Theory, Educational Testing, Item Response Theory, Mental Tests, Psychological Tests, Psychometrics

Reference Table for Basic Symbols and Their Variations

Basic Symbols		
Symbol	Name and case	Meaning
β	Beta (Greek, lowercase)	In Item Response Theory, the difficulty of an item
e	Euler's number (lowercase)	Euler's number, the base of the natural logarithm, 2.718
E	E (uppercase)	The error score; a score resulting from error in measurement
ε	Epsilon (Greek, lowercase)	The statistical operator meaning to find an expected value
i	I or index (lowercase)	Index number of a given participant
ln	Natural log (lowercase)	The natural log of a number
K	Kay	Number of items or "segments" in a test
M	Em	The mean of a sample
μ	Mu (Greek, lowercase)	The population mean
N	En (uppercase)	Number of participants/observations
ρ	Rho (Greek, lowercase)	The population correlation
S	Ess (uppercase)	The standard deviation of a sample
S^2	Ess-squared (uppercase)	The variance of a sample
Σ	Sigma (Greek, uppercase)	The statistical operator meaning to sum a group of numbers
σ	Sigma (Greek, lowercase)	The standard deviation of a population
σ^2	Sigma squared (Greek, lowercase)	The variance of a population
T	Tee (uppercase)	The true score; a hypothetical construct; a measure of a person's pure ability, attitude, or trait alone
θ	Theta (Greek, lowercase)	In Item Response Theory, a person's true or latent level of ability
X	Ex (uppercase)	A test, X, or raw scores on test X; the observed score; the actual score an individual gets
x	Ex (lowercase)	Deviation scores on test X
Y	Wy or wye (uppercase)	A test, Y, or raw scores on test Y
y	Wy or wye (lowercase)	Deviation scores on test Y
z	Zee or zed (lowercase)	z-scores

(*Continued*)

Reference Table for Basic Symbols and Their Variations (*Continued*)

Variations on the Basic Symbols		
Symbol	**Read as**	**Meaning**
X'	"ex prime"	The observed scores on a test parallel to test X
T'	"tee prime"	The true scores on a test parallel to test X
E'	"e prime"	The error scores on a test parallel to test X
$\rho_{XX'}$	"rho sub x x prime"	All of these are expressions for test reliability
ρ^2_{XT}	"rho squared sub x t"	
ρ_{XX}	"rho sub x x"	
σ^2_X	"sigma squared sub x"	Variance of the obtained scores
σ^2_T	"sigma squared sub t"	Variance of the true scores
σ^2_E	"sigma squared sub e"	Variance of the error scores

Contents

About the Book

Mental tests are used in classrooms, occupational settings, healthcare, and the justice system. Most people, however, have only a beginning acquaintance with how such tests work. *The Elements of Mental Tests* is written to explain how tests measure the key psychological qualities of a person. The book is written for undergraduate students and other interested readers with backgrounds in psychology, education, human resources, healthcare, and the law, and those who are interested in learning about the tests that are often an integral part of their professional experience. The three parts of this book cover the basics of mental measurement, the meaning of test scores, and the foundations of good measurement.

Part I, *The Elements of Measurement*, covers what tests are, how they are written, and some of the psychological principles behind how they work. Part II, *The Elements of Test Scores*, explains in reader-friendly language some key mathematical ideas behind how tests measure what they do, drawing on both classical and contemporary test theory. Part III, *The Elements of Test Quality*, explains the criteria of a good test, including how to decide if a test measures what it is supposed to, and related issues of high-quality psychological assessment. Each of the 12 brief chapters that collectively make up the book are clear, simple, and to the point.

John D. Mayer is Professor of Psychology at the University of New Hampshire where he regularly teaches courses in psychological measurement. He is a coauthor of the internationally known *Mayer-Salovey-Caruso Emotional Intelligence Test* (MSCEIT; MHS, Toronto), the author of *Personal Intelligence: The Power of Personality and How it Shapes Our Lives* (Scientific American/Farrar, Straus, Giroux), and is the author to over 125 other scientific articles, tests, and books. He lives in New Hampshire.

About the Book

Acknowledgments

This book is a product, in part, of the many wonderful teachers and colleagues from whom I have learned. Douglas Shultz, a professor at Case Western Reserve University, provided my incoming graduate-student class with our first introduction to the field of testing—complete with tales of mid-20th century work in psychometrics. Douglas K. Detterman, my graduate advisor, explained the utility of psychometrics for experimental research and its applications in intelligence testing. Sandra Russ, who taught us psychological assessment, trained us in the use of clinical tests such as the *WAIS* tests and the *MMPI*. After graduate school, I was fortunate to take a course from Jeffrey Tanaka (then of New York University).

Around the year 2000, David R. Caruso and Peter Salovey of Yale University and I began our work with the test publisher MHS, of Toronto, to develop the *Mayer-Salovey-Caruso Emotional Intelligence Test* or *MSCEIT*, which was first published in 2002. As part of our work on the *MSCEIT*, I had (and still have) the pleasure of collaborating with Dr. Gill Sitarenios, the Director of Research at that firm. Working with MHS, I learned more about the applied aspects of testing: norming a test, scaling it, and participating in the validation process firsthand. More recently, with Dr. Iris Lin, we have begun work on the *MSCEIT-2*.

In 2008, I began developing a test of personal intelligence—an intelligence we use to understand our own and other people's personalities. On that project, I again have had the opportunity to work with David R. Caruso and with Dr. Abigail T. Panter, an expert in the mathematical models used to understand tests, who is at the L. L. Thurstone Psychometric Laboratory at the University of North Carolina, Chapel Hill.

I have taught a class in measurement at the University of New Hampshire for over 20 years now and over that time I have had the opportunity to hear from many of my students about earlier versions of this book. I'm especially grateful for comments from Chandler Giese, Lauren Guetling, Kaitlin Lounsbury, and Richard Wilson.

Alexander M. Rocke of the University of New Hampshire and Brooke Magnus of the University of North Carolina reviewed key passages in the book related to technical and psychometric issues. Alex went over the material with a keen mathematical eye and pointed out both corrections and ways to make symbols and equations I used more accessible to students. Brooke recommended a number of corrections and clarifications that have improved the accuracy of my coverage of the field. My thanks to them both. Angie Joachim carefully copy edited the work, ensuring it was clearer and easier to read than before. Rachael Cavallaro of SUNY Binghamton University assisted with the references. I am grateful to them all. Any remaining errors in this text are of my own making.

I want to express my gratitude as well to Shoshanna Goldberg, Stewart Mattson, Peggy Williams, Sheri Dean, Charlene Kronstedt, and the many other people at Momentum Press. I also want to express my thanks to those at Exeter Premedia Services, Chennai, India, who helped produce the print and electronic versions of this work. They all have been a pleasure to engage with throughout the process of developing this book.

—John D. Mayer, November 3, 2015

PART I

The Elements of Measurement

CHAPTER 1

The Purpose of Mental Testing

Why Study Mental Tests?

It would be "a thousand times better," remarked the journalist Walter Lippmann in 1922, "if all the intelligence testers and all their questionnaires were sunk without warning in the Sargasso Sea." Lippmann was 24 years old at the time and was reacting to the first intelligence tests introduced in North America (Lippmann, 1922, p. 297; Luskin, 1972). Lewis Terman, one of the intelligence testers that Lippmann had singled out, and a professor at Stanford University, regarded Lippmann's logic as faulty "when it is not downright loco ... ." The professor explained that he had characterized Lippmann's argument as nonsensical in "a charitable way" to explain the journalist's "misuse of facts and quotations" (Terman, 1922, p. 117).

Eighty years later, as the 20th century drew to a close, the science of testing had grown in its influence. Yet the same conflicts between test-makers and critics arose in public commentary. In 1981, the biologist turned public intellectual Stephen Jay Gould wrote *The Mismeasure of Man*, in which he, too, criticized mental testing; there had been many similar critiques throughout the century. Gould argued that a mathematical technique called *factor analysis*, which psychologists apply to understand the nature of intelligence, was flawed in serious ways. John Carroll, an eminent expert in the technique, provided a counterargument to Gould's work, concluding:

> I hope I have demonstrated that in the main, Gould's statements and accusations about factor analysis are incorrect and unjustified, and should not be regarded as constituting an authoritative guide to evaluating this technique. (Carroll, 1995, p. 131)

There is a pattern here: Journalists and other public intellectuals critique mental tests; experts in mental measurement, in turn, are concerned that those critics don't understand how tests work.

Tests Are Consequential

We all have an interest in tests because they affect our lives—hence the media coverage. Almost everyone takes tests: students, job applicants, medical patients, and criminal defendants. Many professionals use test results in their work: psychologists, of course, but also psychiatrists, lawyers, judges, physicians, medical practitioners, and those in human resources.

For example, judges often try to make sense of what they hear from expert witnesses in psychological assessments. In one court case, a father who was involved in a child custody dispute had taken a psychological test and scored in the normal range on a number of scales of mental disorders, except for an elevated score on *Dominance.* The psychologist who testified about the test results regarded the high score as indicating the father had an autocratic, willful character. An alternative interpretation, however, was that the father had the capacity to take charge of his life, establish workable plans, and meet deadlines (Underwager & Wakefield, 1993). Judges who lack an understanding of psychological tests may be confounded by such conflicting interpretations, often unable to follow evidence for the test and its interpretation (Kleiman & Faley, 1985).

The Aim of This Book

Despite the importance of testing to public policy, very few people understand how tests work. The responsibility for evaluating tests and what they do has fallen chiefly on the small group of individuals known as psychometricians, and those sufficiently well-trained to read their writings.

In this book, I provide an introduction to what mental tests are and to how they work, so that seriously interested individuals can better judge the merits of such measures. Most of my readers will likely be undergraduate students taking their first course in psychological measurement. That said, the book also has been developed for allied professionals and other readers who are interested in the topic. I have made every effort to carefully explain the elements of tests, keeping in mind that many of my readers may have little knowledge of testing other than the tests they have taken.

In the coverage of mathematical aspects of testing (chiefly in Chapters 5 through 10), I have taken special care to remember that my readers may have little or no experience of what I will discuss. I have tried to explain everything as clearly as possible. Readers can choose to skip many of the equations and focus on the explanations in the narrative. Most of the math through Chapter 8 is expressed as very simple algebra. In Chapter 9, I introduce Item Response Theory, and that necessitates equations for curves based on the logarithms of odds ratios ("logits"). There also, readers who prefer to rely on the narrative can skip the equations and focus on the accompanying explanations to make sense of the technique.

What Is a Mental Test?

To understand mental tests, it helps to have a starting definition of what one is. For easy reference, I have offset the definition we will use here:

> A mental test is an integrated measurement procedure that collects data about one or more features of an individual's mental life, and uses that data to assign a score or scores indicating the presence or magnitude of those features of the individual.

The *mental* part of the mental test refers to a person's psychological features: matters such as motives and emotions, knowledge and intelligences, social acts, and self-control. Blood tests or measures of physical capacity would not typically be included, although they may be considered tests of another kind—and many of the same rules for tests discussed here also apply to those assessments.

The *measurement procedure* refers to a standard and well-defined process of collecting data relevant to the person's mental life. Consider the Rorschach inkblots: 10 inkblots chosen by Hermann Rorschach and his publisher and reproduced on glossy cards. Psychologists show their clients the cards and ask what they see in them. The inkblots themselves are not a test. In fact, Rorschach had time to develop only a preliminary scoring system before he died in 1922—just a year after having introduced his innovative inkblot technique. Through the 1960s, many psychologists preferred to use the blots as a kind of structured conversation with their clients, rejecting any standard approach to scoring. Instead, they formed qualitative impressions of their clients' responses based on Freudian or other theories. Used this way, the Rorschach cards were a measurement procedure (they could be used to collect data), but because there was no scoring system, the cards were not a test.

Psychologists did, however, develop new scoring systems for the Rorschach. In the 1970s, John Exner assembled what he called the *Comprehensive System* for scoring the Rorschach inkblots. It provides a complete and systematic set of instructions for how to turn test-takers' responses to the inkblots into a set of quantified scores. Together, the Rorschach inkblots and the Exner Comprehensive System make a test: the *Exner–Rorschach*, so to speak.

Why Use Tests?

But why test? If tests are difficult to construct (they often are), and require a bit of study to understand, and strike people as impersonal, why not use a résumé or an interview and skip testing altogether? Here are some answers—arranged as several points—in response to that quite reasonable question.

Point 1: Psychological Tests Make Psychology Tangible

The first reason for tests is that *mental tests make psychology tangible.* By this, I mean that there cannot be a science of psychology, of psychiatry, or of education without the capacity to measure features of an individual's psychological qualities. Those psychological qualities and their effects surely exist, but are invisible to the naked eye—much as heat, gravity, or the processing speed of a computer cannot be directly observed.

Science cannot progress without measures for what it studies. Physicists need to measure heat and gravitational force. Chemists wish to measure the energy of a reaction. Biologists chart the growth rate of cells in a culture. Physicians send out blood and tissue samples to be analyzed and assessed by laboratory technicians. Those sciences each require measurement to further their research agendas—and to meet their applied goals.

In psychology, psychiatry, and education, mental test scores represent a key index of the psychological lives of individuals. Measurements allow for comparisons of attributes across people, and for an understanding of what an attribute such as a need for excitement might predict about a person across the lifespan. Such tests take a human quality that cannot be directly observed and then quantify it with a test score to make it tangible.

Point 2: Psychological Tests Outperform Other Means of Measurement

Another reason to test is that *tests often outperform even highly trained professionals* in assessing an individual's personality and in predicting the consequences of possessing certain personality characteristics.

To pick one example, consider the test as a selection instrument for a job. A common alternative to tests when hiring someone is the employment interview. In a traditional interview, the individual and the interviewer sit down together and have a talk. Typically, the interviewer asks questions and the applicant answers them, and then the interviewer makes a decision as to how well the candidate would fit the job.

The interview process certainly can be a warmer, more personal process than the test process—at least if the applicant gets along with the interviewer and believes there is some chance he will get the job. But how does the interview process compare with the measurement of a test in terms of accurately evaluating the applicant? Not always so well, it turns out.

Interviewers are not always attentive and consistent, even when trying to do their best. Their attention may wander due to factors such as on-the-job pressures or distractions at home. Studies further indicate that interviewers often fail to agree with one another. Agreement, in this instance, is evaluated in terms of a correlation between two interviewers. (A correlation ranges from −1.0 to 1.0. A value of *0* indicates no relationship, and as the coefficient rises from 0 to 1.0, agreement rises.) Interviewers' judgments of a candidate have a correlation of about $r = .37$.

Such a figure would be considered disastrously low for most tests; multiple similar test-based assessments of a person typically correlate at levels between $r = .70$ to .95. Moreover, the $r = .37$ figure is often considered an *overestimate* of interviewers' consistency (Conway, Jako, & Goodman, 1995; Judge, Higgins, & Cable, 2000, p. 385). The low agreement among interviewers means that if they are searching out the right qualities in the applicant to predict on-the-job success, they are doing so only sporadically, and with a great number of mistakes.

Why are interviewers so unreliable? There are several answers. Interviewers tend to make very quick judgments: Sixty percent of human resources managers polled said they formed a positive or negative opinion of job applicants within the first 10 minutes of a 30-minute interview; 18 percent reported they took just five minutes (Accountemps, 2012). Once interviewers form an opinion, they typically ask questions that are biased so as to confirm their initial judgments (Dougherty, Turban, & Callender, 1994). Then, too, the average interviewer has trouble recalling what happened in the interview, correctly answering only about 50 percent of the fact-based questions after watching a videotaped interview (Carlson, Thayer, Mayfield, & Peterson, 1971).

Interviewers also weigh negative information about twice as heavily as positive information in forming judgments about the interviewee; for that reason, the unstructured interview sometimes has been called a *search for negative evidence* (Rowe, 1989). Professionals in human resources may also be negatively disposed by an applicant's physical appearance. For example, moderately obese applicants, particularly women, are discriminated against in experimental settings (Pingitore, Dugoni, Tindale, & Spring, 1994).

Whom do the interviewers prefer? Slender, attractive people who are good at flattering the interviewer, who describe themselves in a positive light, and whom the interviewer perceives to be similar to him- or herself—the same gender, race, and religion (Cable & Judge, 1997; Higgins, Judge, & Ferris, 2003; Judge et al., 2000, p. 384). These biases may not be the best way to choose capable employees.

Some people make better hiring decisions than others, of course. Certain interviewers who watched a videotaped interview recalled most or all of what the individual said and did (as opposed to the average recall of 50 percent). Yet interviewers may change, being influenced by personal matters, or simply improving or worsening at the skill over time.

Few people enjoy taking tests, and fewer still enjoy taking tests in order to qualify for a job. The alternative—an unstructured job interview—may feel more comfortable. When the nuts and bolts of what an interviewer really does are better understood, however, the relative advantages of tests become more apparent.

Point 3: Good Tests Provide a Relatively Unbiased View of the Individual

A third factor in favor of tests is that *good tests provide a relatively unbiased view of the individual.* How are we to find out about ourselves as we truly are? Our parents tell us some things, our friends tell us others. But our parents and friends are involved with us in ways that may cause them to modify their responses, owing to the stakes they have in our shared relationships. When one friend flatters another by calling her "brilliant," is it to be taken at face value or could there be some ulterior motive behind the compliment? When two people get into an argument and call one another "stubborn," who is behaving more stubbornly in the moment? When one person calls another "unsympathetic," who is being unsympathetic? Because other people view us so subjectively, their opinions do not always provide reliable information as to who we are. Good tests can tell us things more honestly than our friends might and more impartially than our enemies would care to.

Historically, the purpose of introducing mental tests was to further social justice. The first intelligence tests were introduced in France as universal education was instituted. The government hoped that such tests would reduce a bias on the part of teachers to favor the children of the rich and powerful. Alfred Binet, who spearheaded the development of such intelligence tests, observed that to be falsely labeled as a weak learner would be unfortunate and that "… those who do not merit it must be spared the record" (cited in Fancher, 1985/1987, p. 70). Since that time, many people who develop tests do so out of a sincere belief that mental measurement tools, for all their limitations, are far more accurate than not-necessarily-impartial observers.

Point 4: Tests Are Repeatable, Observable Instruments, Subject to Ongoing Improvement

A fourth and final reason to test is that *tests are repeatable, observable instruments, subject to ongoing improvement.* Ask people how they came to a decision, and they will gladly tell you what they did and did not do—even though their answers may well be biased by social desirability and they themselves may have little idea of how they came to their decision.

Tests, by contrast, have the advantage of being stable and publicly observable (by other researchers). That is, one can create a test, study it, and then develop a new, improved version of the measure. Joseph McCann (1998, p. 134) attributes improvements to Rorschach inkblots and its Exner scoring system to this ongoing cycle of criticism and improvement, stating "perhaps no other psychological assessment instrument has been subjected to such intense scrutiny as the Rorschach," and arguing that the "major flaws that were uncovered in its scoring methodology directly led to its improvement."

We can't improve our informal observations quite so much because, as observers, many of us simply fail to accurately understand and describe our own judgment-making processes. By comparison, we can revise tests to ensure their continuing improvement.

Why "The Elements of Tests"?

Tests: Hidden and Guarded

There certainly are reasons to keep some features of tests in limited circulation. Keeping the content of specific tests hidden from test-takers helps maintain the usefulness and accuracy of the tests; if test-takers knew all the questions on a test and how they were scored, they could alter their responses to create a desirable impression. This is not a unique issue for psychologists; it would be an irresponsible optometrist who helped his patients to memorize the letters on an eye chart just before a vision test.

With that acknowledged, there is little reason to keep undisclosed the logic of how tests work. The more people understand about tests, I believe, the more thoughtfulness they can bring to public discourse about testing. In addition, I believe that mental tests and assessment should be more of a collaborative enterprise with test-takers so that they understand the principles of what they experience while taking a test.

One reason that psychologists often fail to share information about testing, I think, is the sense that test theory is too arcane and complex to be comprehended by anyone but a select few. There are exceedingly difficult areas of test theory that I acknowledge would be hard for most people to work through absent years of training. Nonetheless, there exists a basic logic to how tests work that I believe can be explained and that most people can understand.

In the course I teach about psychological measurement at the University of New Hampshire, most of my students end the semester with a good command of the concepts of testing, the mathematics underlying test theory, and the all-important concept of validity. The *you can't possibly understand* attitude, which measurement experts have sometimes leveled at journalists and others, can be turned into a *you can understand the basic principles that apply here*, if the tests and the theories behind them are sufficiently well explained.

The Rationale for This Book

This book is for anyone seriously interested in learning about the tests they take, or who thinks someday she or he would like to write a test. I use the book as the main text in my course on psychological measurement, but I believe it can serve as a helpful resource for anyone who is earnestly interested in psychological tests: human resources professionals who use psychological tests, journalists who cover tests, and lawyers and judges who must depend on tests in the courtroom.

The Elements *in the Title of This Book*

The *Elements* in the title of this book refers to my focus on the basic building blocks of tests: the foundations of theory and mathematics that help explain how they work. For example, when I introduce the concepts underlying Classical Test Theory (Chapter 8) or Item Response

Theory (Chapter 9), I have focused on making clear the basics of the topic rather than the sometimes very advanced mathematics that are also important to the field but that are of less interest to anyone but a specialist in the area.

Nor have I tried to survey the dozens of highly used tests available in the contemporary marketplace. Today there are hundreds of educational and psychological tests, each one with its own history, applications, merits, and drawbacks. Studying the most important tests is difficult and limiting because they are now so large in number. Although I will certainly draw on examples of specific tests, my approach is to explain more generally how tests work: the items that make them up, the data on which they draw, and the ways they are scored.

The Strategies and Organization of This Book

The Elements of Mental Tests is a general introduction to tests. The book is not about any specific test, although I do draw on examples of specific tests. I have divided the elements of tests into three broad classes: the elements of measurement, of test scores, and of what constitutes a good test.

Part I: The Elements of Measurement

Part I of this book, entitled "The Elements of Measurement," concerns how tests collect and organize data about people so as to measure one or more of their mental qualities. After the introduction provided in this chapter, Chapter 2 provides an inventory of the types of mental tests that exist, according to what they measure.

Chapters 3 and 4 examine the kinds of test questions (called test items) that exist. In these chapters, I explain how certain test items draw out a person's inner feelings, thoughts, and plans, and extract data relevant to a person's characteristics. Psychologists have developed many kinds of test items based upon the attribute that is being measured.

Part II: The Elements of Test Scores

The second part of the book concerns the elements of test scores. In Chapter 5, the z-score, a nearly universal language of test scores, is introduced, along with a very simple means for calculating such scores.

In Chapter 6, z-scores are related to the normal distribution, and an explanation is provided of why many test scores are distributed normally according to a bell curve.

Chapter 7 introduces the correlation coefficient to those readers unfamiliar with it. Building on the z-score calculations introduced in Chapter 5, Chapter 7 outlines a simple means of calculating a correlation along with a demonstration of how to use the method. The interpretation of the correlation coefficient is discussed. Those already familiar with correlation coefficients can use this chapter as a review or skip over it.

Chapter 8 introduces one key psychometric model, known as *Classical Test Theory* (and as *Classical True Score Theory*). The basic ideas of Classical Test Theory are described, including its fundamental assumptions and a number of formulae that can be derived from those beginnings; the chapter also discusses what the basic theory tells us about tests.

Chapter 9 introduces ideas from Item Response Theory. This psychometric approach examines how test items perform. The techniques involved help ensure that each test item is contributing to the overall test in a way that makes sense. The chapter goes on to explore *latent variables*—the hidden attributes of people that tests measure.

Part III: The Elements of a Test Quality

The last part of the book focuses on what elements make up a good test.

Chapter 10 examines the nature of reliability and the precision of measurement. *Reliability* refers to the consistency with which a test measures whatever it claims to measure. The formulae and algebra for calculating some common forms of reliability are covered, along with what reliability tells us about a test. *Precision* refers to how close a person's test score is to the individual's actual or true level of the mental quality.

Chapter 11 covers test *validity*: how to evaluate a test-maker's claim that a test measures what it claims to measure. By this point, the preceding chapters will have provided a sound basis for helping to evaluate such claims.

Chapter 12 concludes the book with an examination of what makes for a good testing experience. It examines common objections to tests and to the feedback that tests provide, and makes suggestions for improving tests, the testing process, and for educating the public about what tests can do and why they are of value.

I hope you find what is to come helpful and informative!

CHAPTER 2

The Target of Measurement

Helping People to Know Their Own Minds

During the years from 800 BCE to approximately 200 CE, ancient Greeks with a question of significance would make Delphi their destination. At Delphi stood a temple erected to the god Apollo. Within the shrine was an oracle—a young woman from the town—who sat amidst vapors in a cave-like area. She spoke in tongues, probably under the influence of ethylene, a volcanic gas with hallucinogenic effects—and the Greeks believed she could foretell the future (Spiller, Hale, & De Boer, 2002). Here, our interest is on an inscription at the temple's entrance, carved into a column by Chiron of Sparta: *Know Thyself*. This command to understand oneself carries great importance in Western thought. Socrates discusses self-knowledge in his dialogues, and professed to be interested in self-knowledge above all else (Griswold, 1986). But knowing thyself is a challenge.

In his book *On the Soul (De Anima)*, Aristotle proposed that to understand the mind, we have to appreciate its different functions. For example, human beings and animals share in common the faculties of emotions, but not those of higher reasoning, which are more exclusively the domain human beings. The mind must be divided in order to be studied (Aristotle, 1957/350 BCE; Mayer, 2001; Robinson, 1976, p. 48).

Although the command *Know Thyself* on the Delphi temple's column seemed a reasonable injunction at the time, the work of modern psychology has given rise to a discordant response: that self-knowledge is actually quite difficult, and there are many obstacles lying in its way (Funder, 1998, p. 150; Wilson & Dunn, 2004). We can use mental tests to help answer questions about ourselves and to predict aspects of our future based on what has happened to others who possessed similar qualities (Lubinski, 2000).

Mental Tests and Psychological Assessment

Psychological Assessment

Psychologists refer to the practice of learning about a person as *psychological assessment.* Professionals assess people with the aim of answering a specific question that has come up in the person's life. They may recommend the best school for a child, decide if an applicant is suitable for a job, determine a defendant's legal status, or clarify a patient's mental symptoms. Psychologists ask people to take mental tests, and then evaluate their test results, so as to help answer the questions that have been posed.

The Beginnings: Identifying Those with Good Mental Abilities

Governments were the first entities to employ mental tests to assess people's mental abilities. In ancient China's Han Dynasty c. 200 BCE, government officials administered tests of mental ability to prospective civil service employees to make hiring decisions (Bowman, 1989; Teng, 1942–1943). The government hoped to ensure that its clerks could record events accurately and administer the law properly.

In more modern times, the French government initiated work that led to the first intelligence tests. In the late 19th century, a government commission directed psychologists to develop a test that could fairly identify the students who could learn in school. At that time, the idea that all children should attend at least eight years of schooling at government expense provided a radical but important new vision for the country. But with universal education a new question arose: How could communities identify the small number of children who were unable to learn in the new educational systems? The French people did not fully trust their schoolteachers to determine who could learn—suspicious that teachers would be biased in favor of the children of the aristocracy. For that reason, the government stepped in to promote impartial methods for assessing schoolchildren. In response, a Parisian psychologist named Alfred Binet developed a general method for assessing a person's capacity to learn in school, called an intelligence test (Fancher, 1987).

Today, thanks in part to the efforts of such pioneers as the ancient Chinese in the field of occupational testing, and psychologists like Binet, mental testing has continued to expand, and our understanding of intelligence and intellectual disabilities has advanced greatly.

Psychological Assessment and Mental Health

At the dawn of the 20th century, psychologists and psychiatrists also began to use mental tests to distinguish mental disorders from normal behavior. In Zurich, Carl Jung pioneered the use of a *word association technique* to measure a person's inner psychological conflicts. The word association technique involved speaking words aloud to a patient—"mother," "happy," "house"—and asking the patient to respond with the first thought that came to mind for each. Through the use of the technique, Jung hoped to identify his patients' *mental complexes,* defined as associations of emotions and thoughts that caused the individuals' mental illness.

Another Swiss physician, Hermann Rorschach, studied patients in a neurological ward. He experimented by showing the patients a set of inkblots. He had noticed that patients gave different answers to the inkblots he showed them: People suffering from schizophrenia answered in a different way from those suffering from neurological impairments. Rorschach hoped to develop an interpretative method that could help distinguish relatively normal individuals from those who were symptomatic, as well as to distinguish one type of mental disorder from another (Jung, 1905/1973; Pichot, 1984).

A Cornucopia of Targets to Measure

Rorschach, Binet, and anyone else engaged in measurement would begin in the same way: by looking for a measurable attribute of mental life that would separate the mentally disordered from those without disorders. These early test-makers wondered: What is out there that needs to be measured—or that needs to be measured more accurately?

Mental tests are applied to an increasingly wide spectrum of purposes: identifying who can learn at school, who can perform job-relevant tasks, who suffers from a mental disorder, and who is legally competent, as well as enhancing a person's self-knowledge in general.

Basically, any given mental trait or feature—whether it is our willingness to take a risk, our ability to solve complex mathematical problems, or our online behavior—may serve an important role in understanding our mental life. As research advances, psychologists have become more expert at identifying the various mental features that exist and the contributions they make to an individual's personal and social functioning.

There are obviously many places to look for leads about what an individual is like. Psychometricians have mostly focused on measures related to psychological functioning—that is, by examining a person's inner mental life and outer actions, choices, and other behaviors. Today, biopsychological approaches have expanded measurement into brain function itself.

Tests Relating Brain Function and Psychological Processing

Assessing the Brain

Scientists working in the areas of physics, biomedical engineering, biology, and psychology have developed multiple methods for scanning the brain and its functioning: computerized tomography scans, positron emission tomography (PET) scans, and many other approaches. These tests, which bridge the brain and the mind—as well as medicine and psychology—use scans to connect brain activity to specific psychological functioning.

Positron Emission Tomography (PET) Scans

As one example, *PET scans* allow researchers to examine the spread of a radioactive sugar in the brain, and thereby reveal brain-level activity. Researchers first supply their participants with 2-deoxyglucose, a radioactive chemical that can act as a substitute for glucose in the body. Glucose is the central energy source for cells and the body uses glucose to carry out important tasks. By watching the radioactive version of glucose spread through the brain, scientists can tell which areas of the brain are working hardest at a given time.

In one study, PET scans were conducted while an individual visually examined a pictorial display. As the PET scan was taking place, numbers were assigned to represent the level of activity of each brain area (as indicated by the presence of 2-deoxyglucose). These numbers were then used to assign a color code to each brain area. When the area was depicted in yellow or red, it indicated that the brain was burning sugars at a rapid rate; a blue color indicated that the brain area was burning less sugar and existing at a resting baseline. Researchers using PET scans showed that when a participant scanned a visual stimulus, brain activity was highest in the occipital lobe (Phelps, Kuhl, & Mazziotta, 1981).

Scientists increasingly use such measures to study the brain, and the field of biometrics draws on the measurement theory developed here to help understand such measures. In this book, however, our focus is on psychological measures, so I'll move next to the psychological phenomena that connect brain functions to more psychologically elaborate processes.

Tests of Sensory- and Perceptual-Motor Communication, and Supportive Functions

Sensory- and Perceptual-Motor Assessment

Another group of mental tests examine how well a person can transfer information between the external environment and the mind. This transfer of information typically takes place across the sensory-motor boundary: from the outer world to inner mental processes. A number of psychological tests assess functioning at this level. Among them are a broad class of tests that gauge an individual's ability to sense and perceive sights, sounds, tastes, and other sensory experiences.

The Ishihara Test

The *Ishihara Test* for color blindness determines whether or not a person can perceive color. The test consists of a set of color plates. On each one is a set of dots arranged in a circle. Some of the dots, designating a numeral such as *5* or *2*, are printed in a slightly different color from the rest. People with normal color vision can pick out the numeral depicted; those with partial or full color blindness have more difficulty doing so (Foster, 1946).

Also at this sensory-motor level are neuropsychological tests—tests designed to measure the integrity of a person's perception and learning. These tests are often used to evaluate learning disorders, brain injury, deficits related to the normal aging process, and neurological disorders that accompany such diseases as Alzheimer's and AIDS.

The Bender–Gestalt Test

Perceptual-motor tests, for example, are designed to assess how well a person can perceive a figure, such as a polygon or other design, and then reproduce it. On the *Bender–Gestalt Test*, people view a series of line figures and then must reproduce each one on a new piece of paper. People with some form of perceptual-motor deficits are unable to copy even simple figures without distorting them. Such tests can be used to diagnose learning disorders and to help identify specific forms of brain damage (Lacks, 1984).

Using Reaction Time for Assessment

Another sort of test is the reaction time test—general measures of the time a person takes to respond to a stimulus or to make a decision. The speed with which people respond to stimuli is important to everyday tasks such as typing on a keyboard as well as to more rarefied endeavors including how quickly an air traffic controller responds to a passenger jet's altered flight path.

In 1796, the eminent astronomer Nevil Maskelyne, Astronomer Royal, was among the first to use a reaction time test as a selection criterion for his assistants. Maskelyne was carefully charting the movement of stars across the sky at the Greenwich Observatory in England using the observatory telescope. The eyepiece of the telescope contained coordinate lines, and Maskelyne charted the exact time that a given star crossed the hairline. To do this, he had to count off the seconds from the sound of a loudly ticking clock while watching the star move—a fairly complicated mental task.

Maskelyne had an assistant, David Kinnebrook, who performed the same work. The problem was that Kinnebrook recorded the movement of stars almost a full second slower than Maskelyne could. Although Kinnebrook tried to record the stars faster, his speed of perceiving and responding were slower than what was needed. Ultimately, he was dismissed and he returned to his former position as a schoolmaster. Twenty years later, astronomers regularly charted individual differences in speed of reaction to visual events, referring to that as the *personal part* of the astronomical equation (Anastasi & Foley, 1949, pp. 7–8). Since then, psychologists have learned that the capacity to carry out complex tasks quickly, such as those Maskelyne was performing, form one indicator of general intelligence (Der & Deary, 2003).

Beyond Reaction Time

Tests of speed, and of sensory- and perceptual-motor functioning, describe low level but important aspects of mental activity. The designation *low level* means that these processes are relatively smaller and underlie more integrated broader functions of mental life. I turn next to those broader functions.

Tests Focused on Major Areas of Psychology

According to one count, about 400 *parts of personality*—traits, kinds of memories, behavioral styles, and other qualities of mental life on which people vary—appeared in the glossaries of personality textbooks by the mid-1990s (Mayer, 1995). Even allowing for the likelihood that some parts were identical to one another but went by different names, that is a lot of parts. And although I'm not aware of a recent count of mental tests, I'll estimate there are upwards of 2,000 tests that measure people's mental life, with the majority containing multiple subscales, and with each subscale measuring a distinct quality of mental life. Given the multitude of personality parts and psychological tests, it helps to view them according to some broad categories.

Professional psychologists who assess people—clinical and counseling psychologists, as well as those in education and human resources—generally think about their clients' strengths across broad areas of functioning. One way to view these functions is to divide personality into four general areas:

1. *Mental energy*, including motives and emotions;
2. *Knowledge guidance*, including mental models and intelligences;
3. *Social planning and enactment*, including preferred social styles and social abilities; and
4. *Executive consciousness*, including self-awareness and self-control.

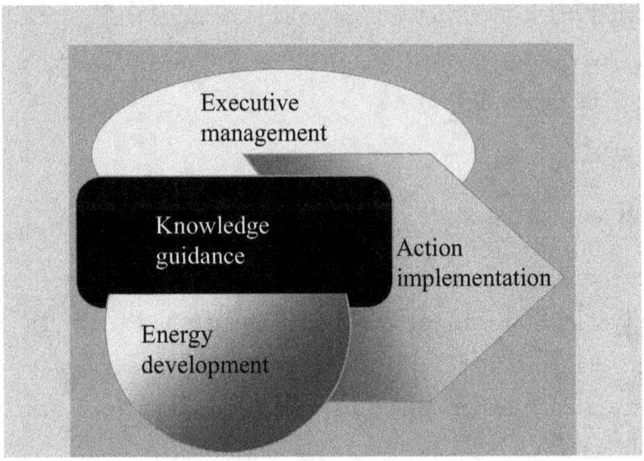

Figure 2.1 Four areas of psychological functions: The systems set division

Note: Personality is divided into the four major areas of psychological function specified in the "systems set" diagram of the personality systems framework.
Source: Adapted from Mayer (2005, p. 300); Mayer and Korogodsky (2011, p. 112).

These four areas, depicted in Figure 2.1, together provide a comprehensive and distinct division of personality (Mayer, 2015). Tests exist to measure each of these areas. Personality tests, in particular, are measures aimed at assessing more than one such area at a time. (Personality tests can be thought of as assessing the broad functioning of an individual's overall psychological system.)

Mental Energy: Motivational and Emotional Tests

Measuring Motives and Emotions

Professionals assess a person's motives or emotional life to understand more about the individual's functioning in those areas. Tests of motives concern an individual's urges and strivings to function in different life areas. Tests of emotions help to describe a person's inner feelings: whether the individual is mostly happy or depressed, frequently anxious, or full of energy.

The Thematic Apperception Test

The *Thematic Apperception Test (TAT)* is a technique that is used to assess a person's motivations. The test administrator shows the test-taker a series of cards with various pictures on them. The many pictures vary in nature from a boy sitting at a table in front of a violin to a couple who appear to be in conflict with each other. The test-taker then tells a story in response to each of the pictures and the individual's motives are gauged from the stories. Sometimes, the TAT and measures like it are referred to as picture–story techniques.

For example, one test-taker may tell stories about the pictures that emphasize characters who want to achieve great things. Another test-taker may tell stories that emphasize good, intimate relationships among the pictured characters. Still other test-takers may recount stories in which the central characters seek power over others. The test-takers' stories are believed to reflect the motivational themes the test-takers perceive in themselves and the people around them, and therefore, to reflect the motivations uppermost in their minds (e.g., McClelland & Koestner, 1992; Smith, Atkinson, McClelland, & Veroff, 1992).

The Positive and Negative Affect Scale: An Example of a Test of Mood

An individual's mental energy depends on more than his or her motivation: A person's motives may be amplified or suppressed by accompanying feelings. For example, depressed individuals often lack the energy to work toward their hoped-for goals. For this reason, measures of mood also are relevant to assessing an individual's mental energy. Psychologists often employ measures of mood and emotional states to assess their clients' emotional status.

Generally speaking, *mood scales* and *emotion scales* both refer to the same group of measures in psychology called *mood adjective tests*. A mood adjective test presents the test-taker with a list of emotions such as *Happy, Sad, Angry, Fearful*, and the like, and asks the person how much he or she is experiencing each feeling at a given time. Examples are the *Positive and Negative Affect Scale (PANAS)* (Watson & Clark, 1997), the *Brief Mood Introspection Scale* (Mayer & Gaschke, 1988), and the *Mood Adjective Checklist* (Nowlis, 1965).

As one might imagine, there are dozens of other measures of mood and emotional states, including general measures of depression or happiness and more specific indexes of shame or guilt. Longer-term moods and emotional states blend gradually into emotion-related traits. For example, the trait of Negative Affect (NA), also known as Neuroticism, reflects a person's tendency to indicate that they feel *Sadness*, *Anger*, and *Fear* on a test more often than average. Among measures of depression, one of the most frequently used is the *Beck Depression Inventory*, a self-report scale in which test-takers describe their negative feelings, thoughts, and physical activity levels (Ready & Veague, 2014). Traits of Negative Affect (Neuroticism) appear on a variety of more general personality scales.

Action Implementation: Tests of Social Action and Social Relations

Assessing Social Relations

Mental health practitioners often want to learn about their clients' relationships as part of their assessments. Tests of social styles, relationships, and social acts have been developed for people of all ages, although they are applied most often in the assessment of children with behavioral issues (Ready & Veague, 2014). For example, attachment patterns describe the sorts of behaviors infants learn in the intimate presence of their mothers (and fathers) at an early age, and represent how the infants relate to their caretakers. Some infants learn that their parents are responsive and trustworthy. Other infants learn that their parents may be less reliable sources of comfort.

Measuring Attachment Styles

The *Ainsworth Strange Situation* is a psychological test of infant attachment. Infants are observed in a series of experimenter-arranged situations. The infant begins in the presence of his or her mother, and is then encouraged to explore some toys, and later on undergoes a brief separation from and reunion with the mother. By watching the infant's behavior, psychologists assess the child's early intimate relationships with others. Infants who explore and play comfortably in the strange situation, and who are able to separate well from their mothers and are comforted by their mothers in a reunion are said to possess a secure attachment style. By comparison, infants who are distressed by a separation from their mothers and then avoid the reunion with their mothers, may be classified as having an anxious–avoidant or other attachment style (Ainsworth, Blehar, Waters, & Wall, 1978).

Infant attachment provides a foundation for later adult attachment behavior. Bartholomew and Horowitz (1991) developed a measure of adult attachment styles that roughly draws on the same secure, anxious, or avoidant qualities of interacting with others.

Extraversion as a Social Style

Professionals may also measure their client's extraversion, a social quality that reflects how much a person engages in lively socializing versus the degree to which the individual prefers to be alone, called introversion. Extraversion is relatively simple and quick to assess. Scales typically include questions such as "Do you like to be in a situation with plenty of excitement and activity?" "Can you regularly add some life into a dull party?" and "Do you like to mix socially with people?"—all of which represent the extroverted side of matters (Eysenck & Eysenck, 1963). Scales of extraversion often are included in more global measures of personality traits (a subject covered near the conclusion of this chapter).

Knowledge Guidance: Mental Models and Intelligences

Thinking About Education and Intelligence

Educational psychologists are often asked questions about the cognitive functioning of their clients. Schools ask, "Is this child able to function intellectually in a typical classroom?" Physicians faced with patients who seem unable to take care of themselves may inquire, "What is this patient's level of intelligence?" And colleges try to assess, "If accepted, will this applicant succeed at our institution?"

We use what we know to guide our behavior. This *knowledge guidance* area is illustrated in Figure 2.1 (center). To guide ourselves, we use both the knowledge we have acquired to function in society and our intelligence, with which we reason. From this perspective, a person's knowledge and intelligence are both keys to guiding her through the challenges of everyday living.

Societies make enormous efforts to school their young people. Students' academic preparation is of great importance to their finding employment in business, government, and other organizations. Societies reward people who have achieved higher levels of education and who are capable of using the best, most accurate models of the world that experts have developed (Cheeseman Day & Neuberger, 2002). Educators and politicians rely on tests to assess not only what individuals learn but also how well schools perform.

Educational Assessments

Educational tests themselves come in several broad varieties—from everyday classroom tests to more ambitious curriculum-based achievement tests that are developed by government agencies, often in cooperation with private consultants.

Almost everyone reading this book will have taken many classroom tests. Like other educational assessments, classroom tests may measure the basic abilities to read, write, perform arithmetic, and they may assess students' formal knowledge of subject areas including geography, history, and branches of science.

A more formal type of educational test is the academic achievement test, which is designed to assess a child's overall learning over the space of one or two years' time. These achievement tests generally produce specific scores for several broad subject areas, such as history, English, mathematics, social studies, and science, and they provide students and their parents with an index of an individual's academic standing relative to her peers. Examples of such tests include the *Iowa Tests of Basic Skills* and the *Stanford Achievement Tests* (Hall, 1986).

Intelligence Testing

A third kind of test in this area, *intelligence tests*, are designed to help understand a person's potential to learn under a variety of conditions. Perhaps the most widely used measures of intelligence in the United States are the Wechsler tests of intelligence such as the *Wechsler Adult Intelligence Test—IV* (Ready & Veague, 2014). There are also measures of other kinds of intelligence such as emotional intelligence (Mayer, Salovey, & Caruso, 2008).

Intelligence tests measure a person's aptitude to acquire knowledge and reason with it well. Research over the past century has secured their position as among the most important predictors of school achievement and many forms of occupational success (Lubinski, 2004; Nisbett et al., 2012). Measures of intelligence reliably appear among the top 10 tests that graduate schools of psychology train their students to administer.

Executive Consciousness: Tests of Self-Awareness and Self-Control

Introduction to Self-Control

Psychologists and those in related disciplines are also interested in assessing people's self-control. If a person lacks self-control, she won't be able to organize and apply her motives and emotions, thoughts, and social skills to operating effectively in the world. Measures of self-control assess a person's capacity to manage unpleasant moods, delay gratification, and avoid impulsive decisions.

Experimental Measures of Self-Control

A well-known experimental measure of self-control is sometimes referred to as the *marshmallow test*; this assesses preschooler's capacity to delay gratification (Mischel & Ebbesen, 1970). Researchers studied how long children could stay by themselves in front of a food treat (a pretzel in the original study) without eating it. Children were told that if they called the experimenter right away they could eat the treat immediately. If the child waited more patiently for the experimenter to return, however, he would get his most preferred treat (for example, an animal cracker). A number of children were very creative in inventing ways to wait. Some talked animatedly to themselves, others sang songs aloud or tapped, and one child succeeded in falling asleep. Those who were best able to wait were regarded as exhibiting greater self-control. Remarkably, the preschooler's degree of control predicted their key developmental characteristics demonstrated *10 years later*. Adolescents who had waited longer for the treats as preschoolers were significantly more verbally fluent, better able to concentrate, exhibited better planning skills, and better social competence (Mischel, Shoda, & Peake, 1988).

Tests of Overall Personality

An Overview of Personality Tests

Tests of overall *personality* measure multiple psychological areas together. The term *personality* refers to the integrated action of the major psychological subsystems of an individual; that is, how an individual organizes his energy, knowledge guidance, social action, and self-control. Psychologists employ global measures of personality to depict an individual's overall psychological functioning—measuring multiple areas of functioning together. Personality tests represent the broadest, most comprehensive level of measurement of the individual. General measures of personality examine mostly normal, everyday personality traits across many areas of functioning. Measures of psychopathology, by comparison, examine personality for possible psychiatric symptoms and disorders.

General Measures of Personality

General measures of personality contain scales to measure multiple areas of an individual's psychological functioning—from motivation to self-control. Professionals may interpret just one scale score, for example, a person's extraversion; but more commonly, the professional takes the configuration of scores into account, using the global pattern—high in extraversion, low in conscientiousness and low in agreeableness, for example—as an indicator of the test-taker's psychological functioning.

A given personality inventory cannot sample every aspect of a person's psychology because there are simply too many parts of the mind to assess. For that reason, test-makers employ some theoretical foundation to help them choose the most important attributes to assess.

One group of test-makers employs the *lexical hypothesis* for guidance—the idea that the most important personality traits are embedded in the lexicon (collection of words) of our human languages. These psychologists reason that if the terms appear pervasively and consistently in the language, then the descriptions must be important to people. Research suggests that human languages describe five or six groups of traits in particular, called *big* traits. The *big five* traits include Neuroticism–Stability, Extraversion–Introversion, Conscientiousness–Carelessness, Openness–Closedness, and Friendliness–Hostility. Tests of the big five include the *Big Five Inventory* and the *NEO-PI* (Costa & McCrae, 1992). (The name NEO-PI was initially an acronym for "Neuroticism, Extraversion, and Openness-Personality Inventory"). People's positions along these big five traits predict important outcomes in their lives.

Measures of Psychopathology

Psychologists and psychiatrists also use general measures of personality to screen for mental disorders. Tests that cover multiple features of mental life do a better job of inventorying possible psychiatric symptoms than more narrowly focused measures—and that reduces the likelihood that symptoms are overlooked.

Two widely used scales are the *Minnesota Multiphasic Personality Inventory-2 (MMPI-2)* and the *Personality Assessment Inventory (PAI)* (Ready & Veague, 2014). Both tests have a variety of scales to measure psychopathology. The MMPI-2 has, for many years, been centered on 10 clinical scales, each one focused on a diagnostic symptom category: *depression*, *schizophrenia*, *psychopathy (i.e., psychopathic personality)*, and the like. With the MMPI-2Rf (restructured form), the focus has shifted away from the earlier diagnostic categories toward measures of specific symptoms such as demoralization, somatic (bodily) complaints, and anti-social behavior. The PAI is a scale with newer origins that has a similarly broad array of scales to assess psychiatric symptoms. Both these scales are frequently used in psychiatric settings.

A key lesson these scales teach is that using one scale by itself usually isn't sufficient to identifying a diagnosis. Psychologists and psychiatrists gain greater clarity by examining a person's scores on multiple scales together.

Measures of Occupational Interest

Another group of broad personality tests measure occupational interests. Career counselors and educators employ these tests to assess a student or employee's motives, interests, and attitudes so as to best match a person to an occupation she might be happy with. The *Strong Interest Inventory* uses one group of personality scales to measure people's interests in six types of occupations: the conventional, artistic, realistic, social, enterprising, and investigative. For example, people who like convention and predictability may find happiness as accountants, whereas people who enjoy being creative are more likely to gravitate to artistic careers (Holland, 1997).

Personal Report and External Source Data

Two Kinds of Data about Personality

Data about personality can come from many sources. Our personalities are within us—emerging from neural processes within our brains. But we also express our personalities in the outside world through communication channels such as our speech, posture, computer use, and other activities. This state of affairs is shown below in Figure 2.2. There, personality is

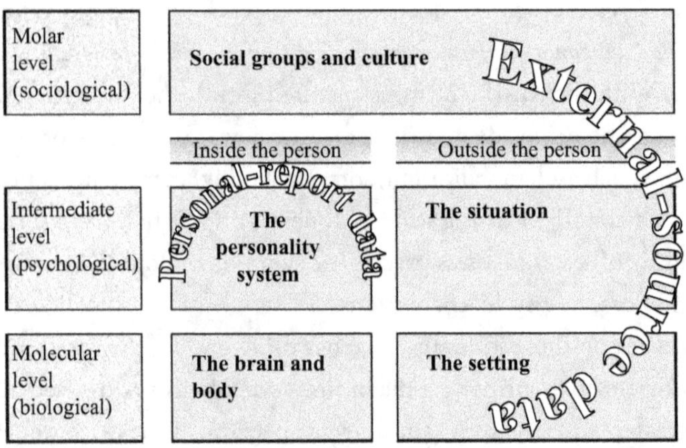

Figure 2.2 The location of personality amidst its neighboring systems (schematic diagram)

Source: Adapted from Mayer (2005, p. 300); Mayer and Korogodsky (2011, p. 112).

located in the center. Underneath it are the brain and body. Both personality and the brain are *inside the person*, beneath the skin. But there are also a number of external systems that surround personality. These include the setting in which a person finds himself—for example, at home, at work, or on a street—and the situation in which the person is involved.

For example, if you meet a neighbor on the street, your personality is within yourself, but you express it in a setting—on the street—and in the situation of greeting a neighbor and catching up on some local news. Also, both you and your neighbor are part of a social group—your neighborhood and more generally your city and nation.

The depiction in Figure 2.2 suggests that there is a fundamental division we can draw between two kinds of data. Personal report data come from the individual herself; as the term implies, it is reported by the person. For example, if we ask a person whether she is happy, her answer is a personal report. By comparison, external source data come from any of the areas surrounding personality. For example, we can learn about a person by visiting her home, which provides us with data from her setting; we can learn by talking to the person, which allows us to observe and form an impression of her from the situation, and we can gather information about the person from her group memberships, for example, that she was brought up as a Hindu and now lives in Austin, Texas. All this is external source data.

Personality's Expressions and Tests That Measure It

The tests we have discussed thus far rely mostly on personal report data, but test-makers also measure characteristics of the person using external sources. Some forms of rating scales ask outside observers to evaluate a target person by observing the target within a situation and over a period of time. Tests of the *big five* traits are typically filled out by the individuals themselves, but sometimes observers fill them out to obtain a sense of how the person appears to others in social situations.

Biodata scales (short for *biographical* data scales), also known as life-space scales, ask people to describe their real-world activities: events from their lives, relationships with other people, clubs they belong to, and even what is in their refrigerators (Mayer, Carlsmith, & Chabot, 1998).

Although this data is personal report (because the target person reports it himself), it reflects the person's outer world. Correlating aspects of personality with the life space helps to explain how mental characteristics are expressed in real-life environments. For example, Gosling, Ko, and Mannarelli (2002) found that conscientious office workers had cleaner, more organized desks than people who were more careless. To do so, they brought independent observers to inspect the same actual offices—and then rate the office dwellers as to their conscientiousness. In this case, the setting, as judged by independent observers, verified the office dwellers' self-evaluations of their conscientiousness.

What Do We Measure When We Measure a Person?

Measuring Attributes, not Entities

The characteristic that a test assesses—such as a specific trait—can be referred to as its *target of measurement.* Note that we never measure an object, but always the *property* of an object: We never measure a table; rather, we measure a table's length. We don't measure a diamond, but rather we measure the *weight* or the *color* of a diamond. Finally, we don't measure an office, but how big it is—or how orderly or messy it is (Lorge, 1951). A property or attribute of an object is any characteristic on which the members of a set can vary. In psychological measurement, we measure the *intelligence*, *extraversion*, or the *conscientiousness* of a person. Characteristics such as these, which vary across people, are regarded as research variables.

Traits as Attributes

Psychological tests measure attributes that include reaction time, motives for power, negative emotionality, intelligence, and self-control, just to mention a few. Psychologists think of many of those qualities as mental traits. By a *mental trait*, psychologists mean a distinct, stable pattern of psychological functioning. Most traits develop as a combination of biological predispositions and learned features. *Extraversion*, for instance, often is viewed as combining a biopsychological tendency toward lively energy, with learned behaviors such as how to socialize and have fun at a party. The key feature of a mental trait is that it represents a consistent aspect of an individual's mental life: in the case of extraversion, the tendencies to seek out other people and to be sociable. Traits can be distinguished from mental states, which are shorter-term characteristics of a person, such as a passing mood. Although some tests are designed to measure states, most measure traits.

The Language of Personality Traits

There are many different classes or types of traits. Some traits describe motives, some describe emotions, and some describe cognitive functioning. Over the years, people have come to discuss many different kinds of traits. Table 2.1 introduces some classifications of traits into the areas of mental functioning they describe. For example, *mental ability traits* describe intellectual functioning and *emotional traits* describe emotional functioning.

Table 2.1 Traits categorized according to the area of mental functioning

Trait names	Description
Ability traits	Traits that describe mental abilities. *Examples*: Verbal–propositional intelligence, spatial intelligence, perceptual–organizational intelligence, divergent thinking, creativity, and social skills.
Emotional traits	Traits that describe emotional functioning. *Examples*: Positive emotionality, negative emotionality, mood set-point, anger, happiness, and anxiety.
Motivational or Dynamic traits	Traits that describe motivations and how a person acts. *Examples*: Achievement motive, power motive, and self-improvement motive.
Attitudinal traits	Attitudes about the world and the people in it. *Examples*: Opinions about whether the world is a fair place, whether other people generally are good or bad, optimism or pessimism.
Personality traits	Technically, personality traits include any of the above kinds of traits. Less technically, the term often refers to any wide-ranging group of traits that are studied as a set. *Example*: the *big five*.

Table 2.2 Formal qualities of traits

Trait categories	Description
Big traits	Broad descriptions of a person's mental life that can be broken down into more specific qualities. For example, the big trait of *neuroticism* can be divided into more specific attributes such as *anxiety*, *hostility*, and *reactive mood.*
If-then traits or *conditional traits*	Traits that are expressed only under specific conditions. For example, a child's aggression would be conditional if he expressed verbal aggression only toward adults, and was mostly friendly and calm with his peers.
Traitedness	Some psychologists believe that only some people can be described in terms of standard personality traits. For example, some people are plainly extroverts, exhibiting sociability and liveliness, and other people are clearly introverts, exhibiting a preference for solitary activities. These individuals are *traited* for extraversion–introversion. Other people, however, may be *non-traited* in that they don't think about the world in terms of extraversion or introversion; rather, they may be *happy* (or *unhappy*) under either circumstance and are inadequately described by the continuum.
Cardinal traits	This mostly historical concept dates back to the 1930s and addresses a possible central trait from which a person's remaining traits develop. For example, a person who is self-centered might as a consequence develop qualities such as stinginess, materialism, forgetfulness of others' birthdays, and the like.

Table 2.2 describes more formal qualities of traits such as whether they are *big* (as in the big five), conditional, or possess some other quality.

Measures as Indicators of Traits

In the past, tests were sometimes labeled *samples of behavior* (Anastasi & Foley, 1949). When we measure something mental, we sample something about a person. It can be his appearance or organizational status—it's not always behavior. We are rarely measuring the mental quality directly. Rather, we infer the trait from the questions we ask. For example, we ask whether a person likes parties and from his answers decide how extroverted he is; we may not be directly interested in parties per se.

An analogy to measuring temperature may help here. When we measure heat with a mercury thermometer, we are not directly interested in the height of mercury in a glass tube, but in what it tells us about the temperature. Similarly, when we measure a mental quality, we are not interested in the test responses per se as much as we are in what they tell us about the mental qualities of the individual. We typically use the individual's responses on a test to draw conclusions about the internal mental quality that is targeted.

The responses people make on a test are generally in response to the individual questions on the test. These questions are called test *items*. The next two chapters examine a variety of these items and how they work.

CHAPTER 3

Just Asking: Self-Judgment and Process-Report Test Items

Exploring Inside the Person

The first test developers hoped that their new measures would allow them to explore inside people's minds so as to better understand how test-takers felt and thought. At the outset of the 20th century, psychologists unveiled new mental measures that promised to fulfill their aspirations. Hermann Rorschach developed the Rorschach inkblot test as a means to "penetrate by way of the test into the world of the mentally ill ..." (cited in Paul, 2004, p. 20). Although the test was innovative and marked a step forward, later research would temper his hopes. Nonetheless, since Rorschach's time, psychological measurement has advanced in a number of important ways.

This chapter and the next examine a key element of psychological tests: the questions that appear on them, which are known as *test items*. These test items come in many forms, and the queries they pose to test-takers are broad and varied both in terms of what they ask and how they ask them.

Types of Test Items: Their Coverage in This Chapter and the Next

In both Chapters 3 and 4, I will focus on personal-report data—that is, items filled out by the test-taker him- or herself—as opposed to observer ratings and institutional data. I'll begin this chapter by looking at some of the simplest forms of items, *process-report items* and *self-judgment items*, both of which elicit a person's own reports. These items pose questions that draw on people's cognition in distinct ways; as a consequence, they draw out subtly different types of information (Mayer, 2004a). The idea that different item types yield different sorts of data will be true for the other classes of test questions explored here. Each kind of item has its own logic and its own strengths and weaknesses. In Chapter 4, I'll examine several other kinds of items, including *criterion-scored item types* and *thematic-response item types*.

Writing Test Items That People Will Answer

If you want to find something out from a person, it makes sense to ask the person directly, using straightforward questions. Many test items ask people questions such as: "What are you thinking now?" or "Are you a lively person?" Under some conditions, people know the answers to the questions and provide them. But many people find questions about their private beliefs, thoughts, sexuality, and life mistakes off-putting. Questions such as "Do you attend religious services every day?" "Are you constantly distracted by sexual thoughts?" and "Have you ever thought of killing someone?" are likely to raise test-takers' hackles. Test-makers may try to omit such questions—even though they may be relevant to certain psychological issues. From an ethical standpoint, they may want to avoid pressuring the test-taker to answer questions that can be uncomfortable to think about. From a practical standpoint, if test questions become too intrusive, test-takers may decline to answer them—a phenomenon called *test rejection*.

In the right context, personal questions can make sense to use. People understand that if they are in a mental health clinic and asked questions like "Do you believe someone is trying to kill you?" or "Do you often have butterflies in your stomach?" on a test, the answers are important for assessors to know.

Certain mysterious and unusual questions may also be acceptable so long as there aren't too many of them: Test-takers are likely to give a test the benefit of the doubt when they encounter a couple of items like "Do you prefer cooked carrots to raw carrots?" and "Do you like science magazines?" Writing test items that appear relevant, clear, and not too personal is the best strategy for keeping the test-taker engaged.

Process-Report Items

Defining Characteristics

Process-report items ask people to report the mental events and processes going on within their minds at the time of the test, as best as the test-takers can discern them. For example, a person might be asked to talk aloud as he tries to solve a complex problem. Such an approach allows the researcher to track the problem-solving process of an individual to learn how he goes about carrying out mental tasks. As an example, a person might be asked to multiply 36 by 24. A test-taker might respond, "… 36 times 24, um, 4 times 6 is 24, 4, carry the 2, that is 144 … 144 plus 720 … and 864" (Ericsson, 2002, p. 983). Note that in this sort of measurement:

> …[t]he reported thoughts are not described nor introspectively analyzed into their perceptual or sensory components, but merely verbally expressed and referenced, such as "carry the 2, 36, and 144 plus 720." Similarly, participants are not asked to describe or explain how they solve these problems. Instead, they are asked to remain focused on solving the problem and merely to give verbal expression to those thoughts that emerge in attention while generating the solution under normal (silent) conditions. (Ericsson, 2002, p. 983)

Participants who verbalize their thoughts in the above ways show approximately equivalent speed and accuracy as those who do not; they also solve the problem in the same sequence as others. This suggests that such verbal protocols can provide highly accurate information about mental events in some contexts (Ericsson & Simon, 1993).

Recording Responses and Scoring

In tracking an individual's problem solving with process-report items, it is customary to record an *open-ended test protocol.* A *test protocol* provides a record of a participant's responses to a test or set of test items. In the case of problem solving, the test protocol consists of a moment-by-moment record of what the person says (as in the example above). In an *open-ended test*, the test-taker can describe his or her problem solving (if that is what's being measured) in a variety of different ways. The test-administrator, in turn, is prepared to record whatever the test-taker says—so long as the test-taker remains engaged with the measurement process, as instructed.

Process-Report Items and Mood Scales

A second example of process-report items is the recording of ongoing mood and emotional states. For example, a person might be asked to record how he feels by endorsing items such as *Happy*, *Sad*, *Angry*, or *Afraid* at a given moment in time. This type of process-report item yields *state-report data.* Such state-reports reflect the individual's current mental state (in this case, his mood). Table 3.1 shows a response format typical of a mood scale.

State-report measures are sometimes paired with *trait-report measures. Trait-report*, in this context, refers to a self-judgment of what one is like most of the time. For example, the Spielberger state-trait tests measure both a person's emotional states and their traits. Charles Spielberger developed three pairs of such scales, one each for *anxiety*, *anger*, and *depression*. The *Spielberger State-Trait Anxiety Index* measures state anxiety—the person's current anxiety level—by asking test-takers to record their level of anxiety while taking the test. The corresponding trait-anxiety test asks test-takers about their typical, longer-term anxiety levels (Spielberger, Sydeman, & Owen, 1999).

Table 3.1 Examples of items on a mood scale

How much of each emotion below do you feel right now?	Please choose one alternative (from 1 to 5) for each emotion ...				
	1. None at all	2. A little	3. A moderate amount	4. A great deal	5. An extreme amount
1. *Happy*	1	2	3	4	5
2. *Sad*	1	2	3	4	5
3. *Angry*	1	2	3	4	5
4. *Afraid*	1	2	3	4	5
...	1	2	3	4	5

Although I have categorized state-report items under *response-process items*, these scales could as easily be classified under the heading of *self-judgment items*, which are described below.

Advantages and Limitations of the Test Type

The advantages of the process report are that it allows for direct questioning as to what an individual is thinking or feeling *at the time*—and therefore, without any retrospective memory distortions. The test questions assume that the individual is in possession of privileged information about him- or herself. *Privileged information* concerns internal feelings and thoughts that only she is aware of. Only the individual herself can choose to observe them and accurately report them. In that sense, the individual is privileged relative to the rest of us. Observers can learn how a person solves a problem, or know an individual's mood best—or only—from measures such as these.

It is possible that process-report data would have been dismissed were it not for the careful work of Nobel Prize winner Herbert A. Simon and his colleague Anders Ericsson. These cognitive psychologists worked out the sorts of questions that people can and cannot accurately answer about themselves. Wilson (1994) pointed out that accurate answers arise most often when (a) the individual reports on a conscious mental event, (b) the event can easily be put into words, and (c) there is a minimal time period between the event and the report—to reduce any memory distortions. Thanks to the work of Simon, Ericsson, and others, process-report data now is recognized as a crucial tool for retrieving important and privileged information from the individual. It must, however, be used with an appreciation of the fact that people's knowledge of their own mental processes is often limited.

Self-Judgment Items

Description of the Test Type

Perhaps no form of test question is as pervasive in psychological measurement as the *self-judgment item*. Self-judgment items ask a person to make a judgment about her long-term qualities. This type of data also goes by the name of *self-report*, but I don't often use that term here because it has several meanings that sometimes contradict one another (see Mayer, 2004a).

People acquire knowledge about themselves from a variety of sources: from self-observation, from comparing and contrasting themselves with others, and from listening to others talk about them. Using this information, they build mental models of themselves—representations of who they are as individuals. These mental models are organized representations of the person's own attributes in memory. Self-judgment test items assess the various opinions a person holds of himself: "Are you talkative?" "Do you generally meet the deadlines in your life?" "Do most people consider you friendly?"—and an almost infinite variety of other such beliefs we hold about ourselves.

People's models of themselves can often be accurate. For example, people are fairly good judges of how sociable they are. But just as often, people's beliefs about themselves may be wrong. For example, people are not always good judges of how smart they are. Sometimes the criteria by which a person self-judges cannot be verified objectively one way or the other (e.g., "I understand myself well.").

The Parts of an Item

Self-judgment items (and the tests that use them) are ubiquitous. Given their frequent use, it is worth introducing the language of test items by using an example of a test item of this sort. Figure 3.1 shows such an item.

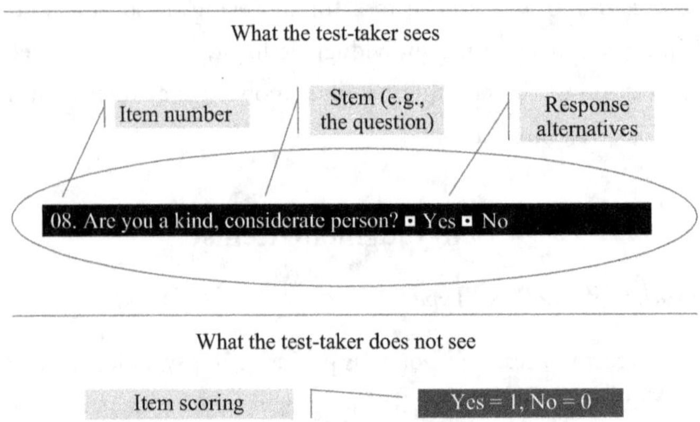

Figure 3.1 Anatomy of a personal-report test item

Test items are numbered. The item in Figure 3.1 is eighth on the test of kindness from which it is drawn. After the *item number* comes the *item stem*—which refers to the question the item asks: "Are you a kind, considerate person?" The stem is followed by a method for collecting the test-taker's response, called the *response alternatives*, which are sometimes arranged in a scale. The alternatives in this case provide a dichotomous choice: yes or no. That is what the test-taker sees and responds to before going on to the next item. The test-maker, however, has decided on further matters about the item: chiefly, how it is scored. In this instance, a *Yes* response is credited with a *1*, a *No* response with a *0*; these values will be added into the test-taker's overall kindness score.

Other response scales are possible. Table 3.2 provides some examples of common response scales for self-judgment tests.

Recording Responses and Scoring

Another example of the *dichotomous response format* used in item 8 (Figure 3.1) is shown in the first row of Table 3.2. Dichotomous response formats are defined as any test item for which the person has only two response choices such as yes or no, true or false, or describes me or doesn't describe me.

Table 3.2 Common forms of test responses for self-judgment tests

Name	Example
Dichotomous Scale	I like parties. (Circle one:) True or False
Likert Scale: Example 1	I am a sociable person: Does not apply to me 1 2 3 4 5 Applies to me
Likert Scale: Example 2	Are you an emotional, moody sort of person? Circle your answer. No 1 2 3 Yes
Guttman Scale	Circle the letter of the description that most applies to you: a. My moods are almost always calm and even b. My moods are mostly calm and even, but sometimes they can be intense c. My moods are somewhat changeable and varied d. My moods can be very powerful, and they change without warning
Forced Choice	Circle the letter of the description that most applies to you: a. I think I would like the work of a mail carrier b. I think I would like the work of a pilot

Test developers often allow people a continuum of responses. Test-takers can indicate not just whether a statement applies to them, but *how much* it does on a *Likert scale*. Likert scales provide graded response alternatives between two *anchors* (Table 3.2, rows 2 and 3). An *anchor* refers to words that define the endpoint(s) of the scale. An example of an anchored Likert scale is: *Disagree 1 2 3 4 5 Agree*. In this case, *disagree* and *agree* are the anchors, and the numbers 1 through 5 form the scale. Sometimes, a Likert scale consists of a verbal continuum, with each point anchored by words or phrases, as in this scale consisting of five alternatives: *Strongly Disagree—Disagree—Neither Agree or Disagree—Agree—Strongly Agree*. Once the participant has made her response, the researcher typically converts the verbal responses back to a numerical scale, which is, *1*, *2*, *3*, *4*, *5*.

Likert scales have two advantages relative to dichotomous scales. First, test-takers often prefer having more than two options to choose from when describing themselves. Second, scales with more alternatives generally yield more consistent (i.e., reliable) responses. Generally, between 5 and 7 alternatives are preferred (Cox, 1980; Nunnally, 1978).

A *Guttman scale* is a scale in which a few statements about a similar topic are graded as per their intensity, and a person chooses the intensity level that applies to him. For example, if the test-maker wants to study friendliness, he or she may create a few statements indicating various levels of friendliness from *I'm a little friendly*, to, perhaps, *I'm a big, kindly, loving, teddy bear of a person*. The challenge with Guttman scales is to make sure that each statement falls along the same continuum as the others—in the example here, along the friendliness continuum. For example, one might wonder whether *teddy bear* is on the same continuum as overall friendliness.

The last type of scale to be discussed here is a *forced-choice scale*. In a forced-choice scale, the individual must choose between two statements about her- or himself.

The two alternatives are chosen such that they both convey the same degree of some socially unpleasant (or pleasant) quality. When the choices are unpleasant, the person must choose between two undesirable alternatives he might otherwise choose to avoid. For example, a person might be asked: "Which do you do more of? A. Lie to someone, or B. Hurt someone's feelings." The format forces a person to own up to one of two unpleasant behaviors that are considered equally negative by most people. Because both choices are equally negative, the assumption is that the person will choose the alternative that more accurately describes him.

Reverse Scoring, Acquiescence, and Similar Issues

Reverse-scored items are often used on scales of self-judgment to avoid issues of biased scale use. A reverse-scored item is a test item that measures the opposite of the targeted attribute and is designed to be calculated in a manner reverse from that of the directly scored items. For example, a test of friendliness may employ questions such as "Most people consider me to be a friendly person" and "I believe I come across as caring and kind to others." A reversed item would be "Most people consider me to be a bit aloof and distant at times." Using reversed items helps clarify that a test-taker really believes he is friendly rather than simply agreeing with all the items. The convention is to write such reversed items with an [R] next to them in any scientific report of the scale, to indicate that their content is reversed. Of course, on the version of the test that the test-taker sees, the items all appear without such special designations. The test-taker (presumably) responds to the reverse-scored item in the same way as he responds to any other test item. The test-maker, however, must reverse the scoring of the item to make the individual's total score make sense.

To reverse score an item, the response is reflected about the mid-point of the scale. For example, the items on a test of friendliness might be scored *Disagree 1 2 3 4 5 Agree.* A reversed-scored item on the test might be something like, "To be honest, I prefer that people keep their distance from me." To score a reversed item for friendliness, the test-maker converts the response scale from *Disagree 1 2 3 4 5 Agree*, to *Disagree 5 4 3 2 1 Agree.* That is what is meant by reflecting scores around the mid-point—the *3*—of the scale. So, if the test-taker responded

1 (Disagree) on the original version of the item, the *1* would be recoded as a *5* and the 5 would be added into the overall friendliness score. The participant's responses would be transformed for a reversed item such that the *1* was a *5*, the *2* was a *4*, the *3* was a *3*, the *4* was a *2*, and the *5* was a *1*.

There are good reasons to use reverse-scored items. First, test-takers may sometimes become rushed and decide to no longer cooperate with testing. Upon deciding that, the test-taker may then circle all *1*s or all *5*s on the scale. Employing reverse-scored items provides a means of ensuring that any such individual will, at worst, obtain a middle-of-the-road score on the scale, rather than an extreme one. That is important, because falsely measured scores in the middle of the range of test responses distort test results less than do falsely reported extreme scores. It also makes possible the detection of such careless responding so as to allow the removal of these individuals' problematic data from the sample.

A second reason to use reverse-scored items is that people may use a given response scale differently, with some individuals preferring the upper extremes of the scale (or the lower extremes) and other people responding near the middle. Balancing out items by using reverse-scored items goes some way toward fixing that difficulty as well.

A third and final reason is that, as already noted, some people tend to *acquiesce* to test items. That is, if you ask them, "Are you shy?" they will tend to agree a little. Similarly, if you ask them, "Are you outgoing?" they will tend to agree a little. Using reverse-scored items helps to control for acquiescence (Jackson & Messick, 1958).

Table 3.3 shows the items of a test of Friendliness. Can you spot the reverse-scored items? How would you reverse score them?

If you chose items 3 and 4 as the reversed-scored items, you would be right. So, a very friendly person who answers *5*, *5*, and *5*, for items 1, 2, and 5 might answer *1* and *1* for items 3 and 4. To score the test, the test-maker reverse-scored the reversed items (numbers 3 and 4), changing the *1*s to *5*s. Had our friendly test-taker chosen 2 for item 3, he would have received a 4.

Table 3.3 Examples of reverse scoring on a friendliness scale

Item stem	Response scale	Reversed?
1. Do people consider you a friendly person?	Disagree 1 2 3 4 5 Agree	No
2. Do you try to express caring and concern to others?	Disagree 1 2 3 4 5 Agree	No
3. Do you pride yourself on using a gruff, business-like exterior to intimidate people?	Disagree 1 2 3 4 5 Agree	Yes
4. Do other people perceive you as unfriendly?	Disagree 1 2 3 4 5 Agree	Yes
5. Do you often help strangers who ask for help?	Disagree 1 2 3 4 5 Agree	No

Empirically-Keyed Self-Judgment Items

So far, we have interpreted responses to the self-judgment questions we have encountered by taking the test-taker at her word: If she says she is friendly, she is.

There is a variation on self-judgment items that interprets the test-takers' responses in a somewhat different way. In this approach, called *empirically-keyed scoring*, people are asked to judge themselves (or others) on a number of different qualities—just as they are in the self-judgment approach—but their responses are not taken at face value. Rather, items are interpreted according to *what they correlate with* or *how they distinguish between groups*.

Empirically-keyed scoring involves a series of steps like these:

Step 1: The test-maker collects a large and diverse group of self-judgment items—typically numbering in the hundreds.

Step 2: The items are given to two groups of individuals who differ in the targeted attribute. For example, if the test-maker hopes to measure depression, one group would have normal moods whereas the other would consist of individuals who suffer from depression.

Step 3: The test-maker would then examine the responses of the two groups on each item and identify any item that distinguished between the two groups—regardless of what the item is about.

Step 4: In the final step, all those items that did distinguish between the groups would be assembled into a scale and scored so that one direction indicates depression and the other indicates a lack of depression. This new group of items (that the two groups answer differently) is the empirically-keyed scale.

Note that if properly constructed, the scale will distinguish between depressed and non-depressed individuals. The content of the items, however, need not have anything to do with depression per se; all that is necessary is that the two groups answer the questions differently.

The most well-known example of empirically-keyed scoring can be found in the original *Minnesota Multiphasic Personality Inventory (MMPI)*, a measure of psychopathology. The new version of the test—the MMPI-2—relies less on empirical keying and focuses a bit more on the content of the items.

The designers of the original MMPI were interested in nine major types of psychopathology that were used to make diagnoses in the 1930s. They collected more than 1,000 items they believed could be useful in discriminating different kinds of mental disorders. They then gave the test items to groups with and without specific diagnoses and built scales made up of items that distinguished between symptom-free and mentally disordered groups.

For example, they gave the entire set of items to those suffering from schizophrenia and to those in a control group who were free of the disease. Those with schizophrenia more frequently endorsed, "Peculiar odors come to me at times," "I hear strange things when I'm alone," and the mournful, "There is something wrong with my mind." Such individuals also answered "false" to "My mother was a good woman" and "I get all the sympathy I should" (Dahlstrom, Welsh, & Dahlstrom, 1972, pp. 216–217). The scale has ended up working quite well.

Sometimes empirical keying can go awry if the groups are not carefully chosen. This happened with the MMPI scale originally known as "sexual inversion." Sexual inversion referred to homosexuality. (Until the 1970s, homosexuality was considered a psychiatric disorder). The apparently well-intentioned researchers were confronted with the issue of where to find groups of gay and straight men at a time when social pressures meant that people closely hid any homosexual desires from all but a few trusted friends.

Accordingly, the researchers identified 13 homosexual male graduate students and colleagues at the University of Minnesota who were willing to take the test. (They were unable to find any homosexual women.) Finding heterosexual males must have seemed easy indeed to the test authors: They simply chose 54 army recruits, assuming that any male in the army would be heterosexual (Dahlstrom et al., 1972, pp. 201–202).

At first glance, the sexual inversion scale seemed to work. A number of items reliably distinguished between the gay University of Minnesota graduate students and the army soldiers. But on closer examination, it turned out that the test authors had confounded a second variable with sexual inversion: The men in graduate school and on the university's faculty were also far more highly educated than the men in the army. Items on the final scale such as, "I think I would like the work of a librarian," "I like poetry," and "I like to cook" were as relevant to educational level as they were to sexual preferences (Murray, 1963).

For that reason, college educated males scored high on the (renamed) femininity end of the original MMPI scale until that first edition was retired: Many educated men liked to read, listen to classical music, and cook, regardless of their sexual orientation (Dahlstrom et al., 1972; Wong, 1984).

When samples are better chosen than in this example and sufficiently large, empirical keying works well—and can suggest new insights. One MMPI test item that distinguished depressed from non-depressed Minnesotans was, "I go to church almost every week," indicating that churchgoers were less depressed. From such findings, psychologists made the connection that involvement in religious communities was one protective factor against depression. To some degree, the test item may have suggested hypotheses and helped to generate research about the relationships discovered, for example, between mood and membership in a community (Keyes & Waterman, 2003).

Advantages and Limitations of the Test Type

Self-judgment scales are among the most widely employed scales in psychology. The standard versions of the scales (disregarding, for a moment, forced-choice and empirically-keyed questions) provide a quick and convenient means of assessing key features of an individual's self-perception. Under conditions where the test-taker can be counted upon to share information willingly, these scales will work well for many purposes. In part, that is because of their ease of construction and ease of use.

Forced-choice scales provide additional controls for social desirability, as do methods of empirical keying. The latter allows the researcher to treat responses according to their actual value as an indicator of group membership (e.g., individuals with depression), rather than taking the item at face value.

Well-designed self-judgment scales usually meet certain criteria of a good test, particularly as regards their consistency of measurement (i.e., reliability). That is, when they are properly constructed, they tend to yield similar scores at different points in time.

Along with those advantages, however, self-judgment tests have serious drawbacks. The limit of self-evaluation is that people can't tell you more than they know. Many of us are willing to describe internal mental processes that we really don't comprehend well. For example, the social psychologists Richard Nisbett and Timothy Wilson (1977) went to a shopping mall with four identical silk stockings in one study (and four nightgowns in a second independent study), and positioned them along a counter. Posing as market researchers, they asked people which stocking (or nightgown) was best and why.

The results revealed a pronounced horizontal position effect. In the case of the stockings, people preferred the right-most product nearly four times as much as the left-most product. Participants explained their preferred choices as having to do with the quality of the stockings themselves, such as the stitching, fabric quality, and color. When asked whether they might have been influenced by the position of the stocking, the authors report, "… virtually all subjects denied it, usually with a worried glance at the interviewer suggesting that they felt either that they had misunderstood the question or were dealing with a madman" (Nisbett &

Wilson, 1977, pp. 243–244). As a similar example, there is surprisingly little connection between how smart a person believes he is and his actual mental ability (self-estimates correlate with actual ability about $r = .20$).

Empirical keying and forced choice can leverage a person's self-judgment a bit past her own self-knowledge, but different approaches altogether may be required to further reveal the mysteries of the mind.

If the test-taker decides not to cooperate with the testing for some reason, or the test-taker is clever enough, he can create misleading profiles of himself. Imagine how easy it would be to appear friendly, for example, on the test items shown in Table 3.3. So, self-judgment tests present a very mixed group of qualities: quite useful in some circumstances and less so in others. For that reason, it is useful to consider further types of items. I will do this in the next chapter.

CHAPTER 4

Trust, but Verify: Criterion-Scored and Thematic Test Items

When Just Asking Is Not Enough

Things Aren't Always What They Seem

In Shakespeare's *Macbeth*, King Duncan of the Scots is at war with a former member of his ruling aristocracy, a feudal lord with the title Thane of Cawdor (Shakespeare, 1606/1936). The Thane betrayed the king by amassing a group of his own soldiers who were battling the king's army for control of the countryside.

As the troops engaged in battle, King Duncan worried about how he had misread the Thane of Cawdor. Before the battle erupted, the loyal-seeming Cawdor had exhibited no signs of the traitorous acts he would soon commit. King Duncan pointed out his error to his son Malcolm, counseling him to be vigilant: A person's appearance may reveal no clues of his devious intentions. "There's no art," the King counseled his son, "to find the mind's construction in the face ..." (Act I; iv). If only the King could have seen into Cawdor's heart, what turmoil and tragedy might have been avoided? If only we could look more clearly into the minds of those around us, how much more might we know?

Lie detection of the sort King Duncan could have used remains a challenging task; the complexities involved in separating truth from falsity are beyond the scope of this book. But we need not always rely on what a person says about himself to learn about his inner secrets (Ekman, 2001).

This chapter follows on the last one by discussing several additional types of test items. The items here can be distinguished from those examined in Chapter 3 in that they don't rely on self-judgment but rather look more directly at the qualities of the test-taker—by examining the test-takers' abilities and (sometimes) non-conscious motives.

In Shakespeare's play, King Duncan himself is murdered as part of a cold-blooded plot devised by his hosts, the Lord and Lady Macbeth. The lessons Duncan passed along to his son Malcolm, however, were not in vain. When the houseguests discover the murder, Lady Macbeth exclaims, "What, in my house?" and Macbeth appears dumbfounded. But Malcolm cannot help but recall his father's warning not to be deceived by appearances. He and his brother flee to the British Isles to sort matters out and to raise an army (Act II; iii). Malcolm and his brother's ability to sort out truth from lies was employed in a high-stakes game; their very lives depended upon getting it right.

High-Stakes Testing

High-stakes testing refers to situations in which test scores affect consequential real-life outcomes. High-stakes testing often occurs in the following settings:

- A school psychologist administers an intelligence test to help determine whether an elementary school student is intellectually disabled.
- A college admissions officer looks over a high school student's SAT scores to determine whether the applicant will be admitted as part of the school's incoming class.
- A family court judge examines the psychological test profile of a parent who is requesting custody of his six-year-old, to assess whether the parent is sufficiently mentally fit to take care of the child.

In instances such as these, test-makers routinely remind people that decisions should not be made based on test information alone; yet in each of the instances, mental tests add valuable information about which decisions are best.

In these high-stakes contexts, tests that employ self-judgment items won't always be of value, because test-takers can easily alter what they say about themselves—claiming they are smarter or more mentally healthy than they really believe. For that reason, test-makers often prefer other kinds of tests (and test items) to address these issues.

People Often Fail to Know Their Own Minds

Even when people answer test items honestly, they may be unable to report accurately about themselves. For example, people are often mistaken about how smart they are.

As we progressed through school, we saw how some of our fellow students misjudged their own abilities. Some students are quite smart but may underestimate their own abilities because they compare themselves to even smarter siblings, have generally low self-esteem, or refuse to recognize their own talents out of a sense of deep humility. Another group of students called *defensive pessimists* consistently anticipate intellectual failure and disgrace so as to motivate themselves to study harder. Although they often end up performing very well in school, they regularly convince themselves that their school performance is dismal (Norem, 2003).

Yet other students incorrectly judge their own intelligence because they cannot tell the difference between well-thought-out arguments and illogical ones. Because they have a hard time evaluating their own thinking, their estimates of their own abilities tend to be inaccurately positive.

Extreme examples of this disparity between self-judgment and actual ability can be found in everyday life. A would-be ship captain set off repeatedly from the north coast of Wales while trying to sail across the Irish Sea from Anglesey in a home-made boat. On August 11th, 2000, he was rescued by British sailors for the 11th time—at a cost of $85,000 to the British taxpayers. His rescuers described him as "clueless." Reporters asked him why he hadn't obtained a skipper's license, after having failed the voyage so many times before. He replied, "I don't need one, I'm far more intelligent." His chief tool for the ocean navigation, however, had been a roadmap (BBC News, 2000).

This leads us to the contribution of ability-based tests and their criterion-scored items.

Criterion-Scored Items

Description of the Test Type

Criterion-scored testing is variously called mental ability testing, performance testing, and optimal performance testing. *Criterion-scored* items are questions designed to measure test-takers' knowledge or mental abilities, for which their answers are compared to an authoritative criterion of correctness.

Teachers' in-class quizzes and exams are made of criterion-scored items. For each classroom subject there exists a standard of performance that an individual must attain. An individual's mental performance on criterion-scored tests will reflect the degree to which the student has met the standard.

An algebra teacher may decide to test for the ability to manipulate variables in one-variable equations by asking: "X = 2X + 3, solve for X . . ." If the test-taker answers "X = −3," she will receive credit, but the answer "X = 2X" will not receive credit. A world history teacher may pose the question, "Which Chinese dynasty spanned from 1368 to 1644?" A student who answers "The Ming Dynasty" will receive a good score for that response; a student who replies "The Shang Dynasty" will not. Similarly, an English teacher may assess his students' understanding of rules of grammar and syntax.

In each case, the instructor employs criteria of correctness to determine ideal answers. These criteria may be provided directly by the instructor herself or through answers in a textbook or other expert reference works in the area.

Classroom Tests, Achievement Tests, and Intelligence Tests

Educational tests mark one end of a continuum that spans from specific subject knowledge pertinent to the classroom to a person's general ability to reason at the other end.

A school instructor typically employs *classroom tests* to evaluate the learning of his students. A teacher focuses on a rather specific body of information—in algebra, solving an equation for X; or in world history, knowing the major Chinese dynasties. In each case, classroom tests will cover material specific to the course at hand rather than directly measuring anything more general about the student's education.

Educational achievement tests provide a more general assessment of mental ability. Achievement tests are designed to assess students' educational progress across a grade level of study. They typically are designed for use across schools, states, and even regional school systems (e.g., the *New England Common Assessment Program*). In contrast to in-class examinations, educational achievement tests focus more on the general knowledge that students must master at a given grade level. An achievement test item for reading might present students with a challenging literary passage and then pose questions about what the author was trying to convey.

The tests that get closest to measuring a student's general ability to reason are *intelligence tests*. Intelligence tests assess an individual's ability to learn information and to reason with what has been learned effectively and quickly.

The three-stratum model of intelligence—also known as the Cattell–Horn–Carroll model—is among the more powerful contemporary models of mental abilities (McGrew, 2009). This model divides human reasoning into three strata or levels. At the top is general intelligence—often approximated by a general IQ score. At the middle level are broad intellectual abilities, and at the lowest level are individual, specific mental skills. General intelligence assesses a person's capacity to carry out abstract reasoning, including the abilities to spot similarities and differences among concepts, and to generalize accurately.

The broad intelligences include general knowledge, which sometimes is called *crystallized intelligence* because it grows and solidifies over years of learning. Crystallized intelligence includes a person's vocabulary, mathematical knowledge, and other foundational areas of information. Crystallized intelligence can be contrasted with *fluid intelligence*, another broad intelligence that involves thinking flexibly and quickly about new problems—an ability to quickly take in and manipulate new information, such as detecting the relationships among patterns one has never seen before. Additional broad intelligences include more specific verbal abilities, auditory reasoning, and spatial ability.

The third level or stratum includes specific abilities that make up each type of intelligence. For example, spatial intelligence may break down into the ability to rotate three-dimensional objects in one's mind to understand how they might look from another angle, as well as understanding how to fold paper to create a specific pattern.

Among the most popular of intelligence tests in use today is the Wechsler Adult Intelligence Scale-IV (WAIS-IV; Frazier, 2011). The WAIS measures several broad areas of intelligence including verbal intelligence, perceptual-organizational intelligence, and short-term memory. To measure verbal intelligence, the WAIS asks vocabulary questions like what the word "generate" means. The test measures perceptual-organizational intelligence with items such as puzzle pieces that test-takers are asked to assemble. To assess short-term memory, the WAIS presents test-takers with a series of digits read at one-second intervals "1 … 4 … 3 … 7 … 9," and so on, and then asks the respondents to repeat them back.

All of these kinds of tests—classroom, educational achievement, and intelligence tests—rely on criterion-scored items.

Criterion-Scored Items: Dichotomous and Polytomous Response Scales

Criterion-report scales take a number of forms. In classroom tests, it is customary for the instructor, who also serves as the test-maker, to present an item stem (i.e., the question) to his students, followed by a number of alternatives to choose from. The number of alternatives for the test item may vary from two to ten or more choices. The two-choice format is referred to as a *dichotomous choice* item, or sometimes as *true or false* (or *yes or no*). Items with more than two choices are referred to as *polytomous*, *polychotomous*, or more commonly as *multiple choice* (or, with humor, *multiple guess!*).

An example of a dichotomous item is: *The capital of France is Paris*—to which the test taker must circle either "true" or "false," depending upon which is correct. Another example is shown in the first row of Table 4.1.

A polytomous, or multiple-choice, version of the same question is shown in the second row of Table 4.1.

Table 4.1 Types of items common to criterion-scored tests

Item type	Example
Dichotomous (e.g., true-false; yes-no)	Is the word *tomorrow* spelled correctly? Circle One: Yes No
Polytomous (e.g., multiple choice)	The correct spelling of the word meaning the day after today is: a. tomorow b. tomorrow c. tommorrow d. toomarrow
Open response	(Presented orally) How do you spell the word tomorrow, meaning, the day after today? Please spell tomorrow ... (Test-taker responds by spelling the word)

One of the issues with dichotomous test items is that test-takers will succeed on average 50 percent of the time by chance alone, assuming both true and false responses are correct 50 percent of the time and the test-taker equally divides her choices between the two alternatives. That high base rate of success can lower the sensitivity of the test item.

Multiple-choice items with three or more alternatives improve this situation by lowering the odds of being correct by chance. Multiple-choice items with four responses reduce the likelihood of a correct guess to 25 percent, and those with five responses reduce it to 20 percent. Few test-makers try to come up with more than five responses per item, because coming up with that many incorrect but plausible alternatives is challenging.

Open-Ended Response Scales

Some criterion-report test items use open-ended responding to allow test-takers to exhibit what they know in their own words. In open-ended responding, the test-taker generates a response in whatever way he regards as suited to the question. Individually administered intelligence tests often include open-ended responses: A test administrator may ask what a word means. The participant responds, and the test-administrator listens to her answer and may assign a score of 0, 1, or 2, depending upon its quality, evaluated with the help of examples published in the test manual.

Consider the question, "What does 'honest' mean?" A zero-point response to this would be "I don't know what it means" or "A good policy." A one-point response might be "A remark that is sincere" since it gets partway to the definition. A two-point response would be "Remarks someone makes if the remarks reflect the truth so far as he knows it." When testing for an important quality, such as intelligence, open-ended responding is often preferred because the test-administrator can get a more complete sense of the individual's mental ability.

Open-ended items also are employed in mathematical problem solving. A classroom instructor might want students to solve the equation $5X = X + X + 45$. One way of asking the question would be to do so in a multiple-choice format, where choices such as 5, 10, 7, and 15 were offered (15 is the answer). Using an open-ended approach, the examiner can ask test-takers to record their work, and such work may be far more diagnostic of what the test-taker does or does not know than a simple endorsement of a multiple-choice alternative. For example, some test-takers may see immediately that 2X can be subtracted from both sides, whereas others may need to employ trial and error to get the correct answer.

As with an open-ended vocabulary item, instructors often have a system for applying points to each response. For example, the teacher might assign full credit for solving the problem through any legitimate means and doing so accurately, half credit for beginning the problem properly but for making an arithmetic error, and no credit for failing to come up with any good approach to solving the problem. Sharing the system with students helps them understand that fair, equitable rules are employed.

Scoring Tests That Use Criterion-Scored Items

When teachers calculate a test score, they will usually add together the individual scores credited for each test item. The number correct is then translated into a classroom grade, often by calculating the percent correct and then assigning a letter grade or adjusting the grade according to a classroom curve.

Summed scores on intelligence tests are typically compared to the scores of other people who are the same age and then adjusted to reflect the person's intellectual performance relative to their peers.

People who study mental abilities generally don't use *reverse-scored* items; that is, incorrectly answered items don't detract or subtract from a test-taker's overall score; missed answers simply fail to increment the score higher. Instructors may, on occasion, threaten to take points off from a total score because an individual's answer is foolish, outlandish, or wastes the educator's time. Although in principle some response alternatives might indicate an absence of intelligence, items scored to reflect a *lack* of insight are not generally used.

Advantages and Limitations of Criterion-Report Data

The key virtue of criterion-scored items is that they reflect the individual's actual ability to meet a criterion of correctness in a given area of knowledge. The virtue of accurate appraisal is that most people are unable to accurately gauge their own skill levels. People often do not know how well they did on a classroom test or an overall test of achievement; moreover, people may often judge their own intelligence inaccurately. Criterion-scored tests add considerable information that would not be available otherwise. Moreover, a person's ability to know things—to reason well in a given subject area—is increasingly important in an information-oriented world.

A further virtue of these tests is their potential for fairness. Most of these tests are open to the scrutiny of impartial observers, and if a specific test item turns out to be unfair, the test-maker can remove it.

Yet another advantage is that these tests cannot be faked for a high score (short of cheating). The only way to do well is to learn the material. Test-takers can raise their scores through coaching, but such coaching is time-intensive. Because coached individuals genuinely improve their knowledge and skills, their higher scores may reflect true intellectual improvement. People could, of course, fake *bad* performance on a test of mental ability—getting a lower score than they otherwise would—but the motives for doing this are limited; few people are likely to make the attempt.

The most obvious advantage of these tests—that they provide new, accurate information about a person's ability—is also, perhaps, their greatest drawback. People often receive results on such tests that genuinely surprise them. Sometimes those surprises are unwelcome—people learn that they are not as smart in an area as they had imagined—and most of us can understand that is not a pleasant discovery.

To draw a comparison with self-judgment scales, if a person agrees again and again with items such as "I don't think highly of myself" and "I don't like myself," he is unlikely to be surprised if the test reveals he has low self-esteem. If, on the other hand, a person answers a number of criterion-scored items incorrectly, he may not recognize the fact and may be genuinely shocked upon receiving his low score. Of course, sometimes people are pleasantly surprised to discover that their test scores are higher than they expected.

Another issue of criterion-scored tests is their length. Because knowledge domains are generally diffuse and wide-ranging, criterion-scored tests are often longer than other kinds of tests.

Convergent and Divergent Scored Items

Most criterion-scored tests—and all the tests discussed so far in this chapter—involve convergent-scored items: Test-takers are expected to converge to the correct answer.

A second kind of criterion-scored item—typically used to measure creative ability—is the *divergent-scored item.* Divergent-scored items ask test-takers to come up with numerous unique, and inventive answers to a question. An example of a divergent-scored item is "How many uses can you come up with for a banana?" The test-taker may well respond with one or two conventional sort of responses: "Eat it" and "Bake with it" and then continue with increasingly diverse but nonetheless sensible answers to the question: "For a banana split," "For a smoothie," "To sweeten a pastry," and then, leaving convention behind: "Used on the ground as a weapon to make someone slip," "To smear on the ground and make a trail for ants," and "To create a yellow dye with." Participants who are able to produce unique but sensible responses (as assessed by independent judges) are believed to have higher levels of creativity than others (Gelade, 1995; Russ & Grossman-McKee, 1990).

Thematic-Response Items

Description of the Test Type

The last type of item examined in this chapter is one for which the participant creates an image or a story from an ambiguous stimulus. I'll refer to these items as *thematic-response items* and to the data they generate as *thematic-response data*. Thematic-response items consist of ambiguous but usually interesting stimuli, such as inkblots, cartoons of animals, or pictures of people, of which the test-taker must provide an interpretation of some sort. For example, on the *Rorschach inkblots*, coupled with the *Exner interpretive system* (more on the Exner system in a moment), the test-taker looks at an inkblot and then responds to the question "What might this be?" To answer the question, the test-taker must look at the inkblot and think of what the image or a part of it reminds her of. For example, a wing-like inkblot might remind the test-taker of a bat or an angel. In a second type of test, picture-story techniques, the test-taker tells a story in response to a picture.

We'll begin our examination with the question "What constitutes a thematic-response test?" This problem is germane because, historically, the test-makers who produced the visual parts of these tests—the ink-blots or photographs—were not always the same people as those who developed the scoring system for them; the scoring systems typically came later.

What Constitutes a Thematic-Response Test?

The Rorschach inkblots are 10 cards on which some artful inkblot designs are printed. The cards were developed by Hermann Rorschach in the early 1900s. Rorschach asked neurological patients to look at the inkblots and describe what they saw in each one. He then evaluated the test-takers' responses according to an initial scoring system he had worked out.

Almost immediately, however, other researchers suggested new scoring systems that became much more popular than Rorschach's own.

For example, a system developed by Zygmunt Piotrowski (1937) became popular among practitioners for a number of years. Some limited research indicated it was useful for identifying concerns regarding neurological functioning (Piotrowski, 1937). Today, many clinicians use a newer system for scoring the Rorschach—the *Exner Comprehensive System*.

Because different systems are used to score Rorschach's inkblots, and because the inkblot cards by themselves are not a test (they are just inkblots), I recommend referring to Rorschach-based tests by a compound name that includes both the author of the scoring system and Rorschach himself. That is, I suggest referring to the *Piotrowski–Rorschach*, or the *Exner–Rorschach*, to denote a whole test: the name then includes both the items and the way they are scored. Using this system, we speak of a family of Rorschach tests—each one with potentially different qualities (cf., Weiner, 1994).

Similarly, the Thematic Apperception Test (TAT) consists of a set of 40 cards, loosely based on early 1930s advertising pictures and original artwork. The test-taker is typically instructed to tell a story about a given card with a beginning, a middle, and an end. The original scoring system for the pictures is rarely used today. Rather, a series of systems for analyzing the motives expressed in the stories are in common use among researchers, notably systems based on scoring developed by the psychologist David C. McClelland. Following the same logic as before, it makes sense to speak of a *McClelland-scored TAT*, where the McClelland systems can be used to score the TAT for motives such as the needs for achievement or power (Smith et al., 1992; Winter, 1998). This scoring approach is distinct from other approaches. For example, Drew Westen (1991) and colleagues developed a scoring system for the TAT that examines people's relationship patterns. As you might imagine, the *Westen-scored TAT* measures qualities different from those on the McClelland-scored versions; although it uses some of the same picture cards, it is a different test.

Thematic Items or Projective Items?

Originally, psychologists referred to tests like the Exner–Rorschach and the McClelland-TAT as *projective tests*. Frank (1939) described test-takers as projecting their personalities on the ambiguous test picture, rather like the images from motion picture films of the time were projected onto a theater screen. Psychologists have begun to deemphasize the term, however, recognizing both the datedness of the metaphor and its inexactitude; the current preference is for *thematic tests* and *thematic items*. Thematic items refer to those that capture a theme in the test-takers' thinking style. Weiner (1994) described the testing process with the Exner–Rorschach like this:

> … it creates a problem solving, decision making situation to which subjects respond as they usually respond in problem solving and decision making situations in their lives … it creates an associational situation in which subjects frequently attribute personalized characteristics to what they are perceiving, thus revealing much about their needs, attitudes and concerns … it is a measure of *cognitive structuring* involving processes of attention, perception and logical analysis and … it is a measure of *thematic imagery* involving processes of projection and symbolization. (Weiner, 1994, pp. 499–500)

Researchers who today use the TAT describe it as drawing out test-takers' mental qualities—particularly motivational-related ideation (Smith et al., 1992; Winter, 1998). Of course, "theme" is in the very name of the TAT.

Methods of Scoring

The Exner–Rorschach system requires the examiner to evaluate many diverse characteristics of a test-taker's responses. The images seen in the inkblots are sometimes called *percepts*, and these percepts can be coded according to a variety of features: Does the person use the whole blot in a perceived image or part of the blot? Do the test-taker's percepts incorporate color from the blot? Does the percept match the contours of the blot to any degree? Are there certain themes involved: for example, do people interact with one another?

Some scores are simple and fairly plain to score, such as the number of responses (percepts seen) during a testing session. Other scores involve a bit more work, such as counting the number of times the individual perceived human movement in response to the 10 inkblots, and then dividing by the total number of responses to the cards.

Evaluating the responses properly requires understanding the *Exner Comprehensive System*, and then checking oneself against raters who have already learned the system. Graduate-level clinical psychology students are evaluated on their skills at scoring the Rorschach in many PhD programs. A guidebook provides examples of previous test-takers' responses with normative responses and non-normative examples for many of the scoring categories.

Similar approaches are used in, for example, the McClelland-TAT systems. Judges learn a system for scoring various motives based on previous test-takers' responses to the TAT cards. For example, the need for achievement would be coded if a person's story contained mention of such issues as: (a) the pursuit of excellence or attempts to meet a standard of excellence, (b) the desire to win a competition, and (c) persistence in the face of meeting a task that posed a difficult challenge. Stories exhibiting the need for power, by comparison, involve characters who (a) seek to influence or persuade others, (b) exert control over others, and (c) protect themselves or others from danger.

Inter-Rater Reliability

The complexity involved in scoring the Exner–Rorschach or McClelland-TAT raises a further issue: that of *inter-rater reliability*, which is also referred to as *inter-administrator* or *inter-judge reliability*. Inter-rater reliability refers to the degree to which two test administrators will assign the same scores to the same test protocol. For example, Exner–Rorschach practitioners must be able to agree as to the scores they apply to a test-taker's percepts—and this scoring often requires sophisticated judgments about what the test-taker was seeing. Researchers therefore must assess the degree to which groups of experts agree in their scoring. Trained judges who score the inkblot percepts according to the Exner–Rorschach system do exhibit reasonable inter-rater agreement on what test-takers have seen (Meyer, 1997), and this is more generally true of most widely accepted scoring systems for both the inkblots and the TAT.

Advantages and Limitations of This Data Type

The Exner–Rorschach, McClelland-TAT, and related measures are unique in the tests we have covered in drawing out the thematic nature of how test-takers view the world. These tests plainly yield a very different sort of data than either self-report or criterion-report data. As such, the tests and the methods they use deserve serious study, further development, and widespread use.

At the same time, the original versions of the tests were developed long ago, and some of their features don't neatly fit the (sometimes overly rigid) mathematical standards tests are expected to meet today. For example, test-takers of the Exner–Rorschach are allowed to make as many responses as they wish to the 10 inkblots—and their number of responses may easily vary from 10 to 50 or more. Many of the Exner–Rorschach test scores are therefore affected in indeterminate ways according to how many responses a person gives. For example, if a person responds to color on the blots twice in a total of 10 of his responses, and a second person also responds to color twice out of 50 responses, should the two test-takers get the same score or different scores for their color responding? In the first case, the two responses represent 20 percent of the person's reactions; in the second case, 4 percent. There is no easy answer to the question. Advocates for the Rorschach rightly note that, although such scoring issues exist, the *Exner–Rorschach* (and other systems) validly predict important personality outcomes.

The question arises, however, of how much better this testing approach could be if test designers solved this problem? For example, Wayne H. Holtzman developed a test of 45 inkblots and instructed participants to make one response to each of them (thereby assuring each participant had 45 responses; Holtzman, 2002, p. 9). It seems likely that Holtzman's cards are better than the Rorschach—and research suggests it is quite competitive in its predictions. Despite such promise, research attention to Holtzman's alternative has been sparse.

Some critics have looked at the various scoring systems for these tests and their complexities, and have argued that their use should be stopped. They argue the tests lack validity (don't measure anything of importance; see Chapter 11). Critics often treat different scoring systems for the inkblots (or TAT cards) as if they represented equivalent tests, and then are surprised by inconsistent findings across published research. A more sensible approach is to treat each test separately.

Thematic tests exhibit considerable promise. Rorschach scores using the Exner–Rorschach system and similar approaches can identify cases of schizophrenia at a level similar to that of the Minnesota Multiphasic Personality Inventory, and yet in an entirely different way from that true–false test (Hiller, Rosenthal, & Bornstein, 1999). A review in *Psychological Bulletin* compared the use of the McClelland-TAT to measure achievement motivation versus findings from self-report tests. The review indicated that the TAT scores outperformed self-report in predicting important criteria. At any rate, the McClelland-TAT provided distinct information from the self-judgment measures (Spangler, 1992).

In sum, such studies indicate that thematic-report data is a crucial addition to psychological measurement.

From Data Collection to Test Scores

In Chapters 3 and 4, I have surveyed a number of ways to draw out information from a person's inner psychological qualities and to assign numerical scores to them. In the second section of this book, I will turn to the elements of test scores and what we know about them. That, in turn, will enrich our knowledge about measurement processes, and also about the features of the mind that such scores represent.

PART II

The Elements of Test Scores

CHAPTER 5

The Universal Language of Test Scores

Knowing the Score

Joseph received a score of 520 on his math SAT (a college admissions test), an 82 on a recent 12th-grade history quiz, and has a batting average of .178 on his high school baseball team. Those scores all are measured on different scales: scores on the SAT range from 200 to 800, the history quiz had a range from zero to 100, and his teammates' batting performance ranged from .150 to .250.

In elementary school, children might be graded using a three-letter system: *S* for satisfactory; *L* for learning, and *N* for needs improvement. The system is designed to be understood by young children and relatively unthreatening to their parents.

In middle and high school, a bit more information is customary. Grade-school students learn about tests that are scored up to 100; that 90 to100 equals an *A*, 80 to 89 equals a *B*, and so forth.

In another example, some baseball fans learn that batting averages in the major leagues range from .200 up through the middle .300s for the very best batters such as Ty Cobb (.366), Shoeless Joe Jackson (.356), and Babe Ruth (.342).

When college students take the Graduate Record Exam (GRE), they may be somewhat surprised to learn that scores on the test are reported on yet a different scale, with an average of about 150 and scores that range from 130 to 170.

The above scales vary in their ranges, the ways they are reported, and their meanings. A batting average of .350 is outstanding; an SAT score of 350 can be disappointing.

The reason that measurement scales vary so much from one test to another is, for most people, shrouded in mystery. This variety of scaling is a consequence, in part, of attempts by psychometricians to tailor their scales to the purpose at hand—keeping the elementary-school measurements simple enough for children to understand, and the GRE scores finely differentiated enough to reflect the precision of the test.

Behind the Closed Door

Most mental measures are based on comparisons among people. Test scores are reported as points on a measurement scale; a measurement scale is a method of arranging the scores—usually from lowest to highest. Mental phenomena vary across people and are defined in part by how much of a given attribute someone possesses in comparison to their peers. By convention, the midpoint of a scale is often set equal to the average performance of a large group of people who have taken the test. In other words, most mental phenomena, including performance in school, IQ, or even the number of hallucinations a person experiences in a year, are most accurately interpreted by knowing what the average person is like.

Here is an exception that makes the point: A person's baseball batting average has an external benchmark—the number of times the person hits the ball. This external criterion (number of balls hit), however, is not terribly useful by itself. If you didn't know that most major league batters performed between .200 and .350, you would not know how impressive a .320 batter was.

For mental tests, there is a frequently used scale of comparison that can be employed to assess any mental feature—friendliness, IQ, conscientiousness, and so forth. These scales are made up of *z-scores.* For a given quality (e.g., friendliness), the mid-point of these scores is set as the average performance of a *standardization sample* on the test. The standardization sample is a large number of people who have taken a given test.

When a person's scores are average, her z-score on this universal scale is zero. If a person scores above the average, her score on the universal scale is a positive number, usually between 0 and 3. If a person scores below average, her score is a negative one, usually between −3 and 0. The scale draws its power from its close relation to standard deviations and to correlation coefficients. It can also be easily transformed into test scales of many kinds—IQ scales and SAT scales among them.

There are good reasons that the universal scale is not directly communicated to the public. First, the scale assigns zero to the average person, and for many people, a "zero" connotes a bad score. Second, half the people who take a test will receive negative scores. As with scores of zero, negative scores suggest poor performance to many people. In addition, many people have difficulty working with negative numbers. Third, the universal scale often states scores as decimals, and most people prefer to work with whole numbers. Therefore, the universal scale best serves as a professional tool rather than a means of communication with test-takers.

Almost all psychological test scores use this universal language. Where they do not, psychometric techniques have evolved to emulate z-scores (this occurs in Item Response Theory; see Chapter 9). The most frequently used tests employ z-scores as a foundation for communicating feedback to test-takers. The SAT college admissions test is based on z-scores, as is the Minnesota Multiphasic Personality Inventory-2, a measure of psychopathology, and almost all IQ tests, including the newer emotional IQ tests. Other scales, such as the classroom test with its A range of 90 to 100, B range of 80 to 89, and so on, can be converted to these universal scores as well—although they rarely are, in light of their more informal nature.

Once the universal language of the z-score is understood, it can be used as a tool that simplifies many statistics and the scaling of tests in general.

How to Obtain a Z-Score

A *Step-by-Step Approach*

Early psychometricians, working in the 1920s before the age of computers, often obtained z-scores in a step-by-step approach that involved filling out a series of columns on a piece of paper. The first column identified the participant with a number (or the person's initials). The second column contained the participants' raw test scores (e.g., Kelley, 1927, p. 48). To obtain z-scores, the psychometrician laid out a new set of columns, one by one, each time entering a basic statistic or a transformation based on the previous column, until z-scores were obtained.

Psychometrics is a *large sample* technique, meaning that a great number of people must be measured to draw statistical conclusions (think about 100 people as a starting point, 300 as preferable, and 500 to 1,000 as closer to an ideal). Consequently, large numbers of calculations were (and are) needed when calculating z-scores on tests.

In the profession's early days, many graduate students spent long days doing little more than adding columns of numbers for their faculty advisors and calculating the mean of these columns, or calculating a measure of dispersion about the mean, a statistic called the *variance*. The psychometrician and his student assistants often performed the calculations on hundreds of participants, which could take weeks at a time.

Here I will revisit the step-by-step procedure they used because it is so simple that it provides an excellent way of understanding exactly what happens to test scores as they are converted to z-scores. We shall examine scores from just a few hypothetical test-takers so as to understand the principles of how the z-scores are obtained. We can offload the burden of calculating scores for hundreds of test-takers to today's computers and statistical software.

Some Conventions Regarding Symbols

The following step-by-step approach involves a number of symbols that will be helpful to preview. Some of these are standard for statistical work, and others are particular to psychometrics. The symbols are previewed in Table 5.1 (see also the Reference Table in the front of the book). Although I will introduce a moderate number of symbols fairly quickly in the next several paragraphs, all of the symbols and terms will be re-introduced more gradually a second time, which will better help you learn them, as I discuss the logic of z-scores.

First in Table 5.1 is N, which designates the total number of participants in the given study.

Next in the Table is i, an index that provides a label for each test-taker. Where there are N test-takers, i varies from 1 for the first participant to 2 for the second participant and so on, until it takes on the value of N for the last participant.

Table 5.1 Symbols used in the case of obtaining z-scores

Symbol	Description
N	The number of observations (test scores, in this case) in the sample
i	A variable indexing the specific participants whose scores are being studied
X, Y	Capital letters, particularly X, are used to denote raw scores
M, $\bar{X}$	The mean of scores for a sample
μ	The mean of the scores for a population
x, y	Small italicized letters, particularly x, are used to denote deviations from the mean
σ^2	The variance (a measure of dispersion) of scores for a population of scores
S^2	The variance (a measure of dispersion) of scores for a sample
σ	The standard deviation (a measure of dispersion) of scores for a population of scores
S	The standard deviation of scores for a sample
z	Used to denote a z-score
Σ	The Greek letter sigma is used to denote a mathematical operation: the adding up of a set of numbers

We will want each person's raw score on a test. A raw score is the person's score on the test scale of interest. These might be, for example, the response to a number of friendliness test items, added up to a total score (reversing items as needed; see Chapter 3). Conventionally, raw scores on test X are simply labeled X. Raw scores on a second test Y are labeled as Y. The mean (average) of scores on test X is designated by M_x or alternatively by M or $\bar{X}$.

Deviations from the mean refer to the difference between a raw score and the average test score. A deviation is represented as a lower case, italicized version of the letter designating the raw score. So, if X is a raw score on test X, x is its deviation from the mean. Or, if Y is the raw score on test Y, then y is the deviation from the mean.

An index of dispersion about the mean is known as the variance, and it is symbolized as σ^2 or S^2. The square root of the variance is known as the standard deviation, and that is symbolized as σ or S. The letter z, sensibly enough, denotes a z-score.

One last symbol to consider is Σ, which is an operator that means to add up a group of numbers. An operator in mathematics is a symbol that tells us to do something; +, −, ×, and ÷ are all operators. Σ, as noted, simply instructs us to add up a group of numbers. For example, ΣX instructs us to add up all the raw scores on test X.

Some Comments on My Use of Symbols

I will generally present formulae using the symbols for population statistics and work out problems using the symbols for the sample statistics. For example, I'll use the lower case μ (Greek mu) to represent the population mean in formulae, and M to represent the mean in the tables. Similarly, I'll use σ (Greek sigma) as the standard deviation in equations and S to represent the standard deviation in tables in which I work out an example. My rationale is that in psychometrics, basic equations typically are expressed with terms representing population values. On the other hand, computational examples—shown in the tables—are most often carried out with symbols representing sample values.

You may recall from your statistics course that sample statistics for the variance and standard deviations are biased estimates of the same values for the population. To correct for this bias, the statistics are often adjusted by replacing N with $N-1$ in the denominator of the formulae (Bessel's correction), which provides an unbiased estimate of the population variance. In this instance, however, I will omit the $N-1$ correction, which is largely irrelevant to psychometric work, in which minimum *N*s are typically 200 or more.

All these choices are compromises in service of keeping the central concepts in focus for those who are less familiar with the material while respecting the conventions of the field.

The Step-by-Step Approach

Now we are ready to calculate some z-scores. In the example to follow, eight people ($N = 8$) took a test.

Step 1: The Participants and Their Raw Scores

We start with our first two columns—the participants' labels, which run from 1 to 8, and each participant's raw score on test X. So, a label for each test-taker is entered in the first column. We could put names or initials here, but that could compromise confidentiality, so numbers are preferred. This is shown in Table 5.2, in the column labeled *i.*

Table 5.2 Step 1 of a step-by-step approach to obtaining z-scores

Index number	Raw score	Mean	Deviation	Deviation squared	Standard deviation	*z*-score
i	X	M, $\bar{X}$	*x*, X–M	x^2, $(X–M)^2$	S	*z*
1	0					
2	8					
3	4					
4	4					
5	8					
6	0					
7	2					
8	6					
Σ	32					

Next, the raw scores of the test-takers are entered into the table in the column labeled X. Note that Step 1 is entirely clerical. Nothing is calculated here; we simply are labeling the eight participants and recording their test scores on test X.

Step 2: The Mean

For Step 2, we first need to calculate the mean of the raw scores using the following formula (Equation 5.1).

Equation 5.1 indicates that the population mean, μ, equals the sum of the *X*s (raw scores) divided by *N* (the number of raw scores). In simple terms, one adds up the scores and divides them by the number of scores. In this instance, the sum of the scores is 0 + 8 + 4 + 4 + 8 + 0 + 2 + 6 = 32.

Equation 5.1

$$\mu = \frac{\Sigma X}{N}$$

where:
μ is the population mean (symbolized as M or $\overline{X}$ for a particular sample),
Σ is an operator meaning to add up numbers,
X represents the raw scores, and
N is the total number of participants.

The $N = 8$ because there are eight different observations. So $M = 32/8 = 4$. To complete the step, the mean is then entered into the third column with $\overline{X}$ or M on top, as shown in Table 5.3. The mean is the same number for each person. It may seem a bit repetitious to do this, but it will help with computations in later steps.

Table 5.3 Step 2 of a step-by-step approach to obtaining z-scores

Index number	Raw score	Mean	Deviation	Deviation squared	Standard deviation	z-score
i	X	M, $\overline{X}$	x, X–M	x^2, $(X–M)^2$	S	*z*
1	0	4				
2	8	4				
3	4	4				
4	4	4				
5	8	4				
6	0	4				
7	2	4				
8	6	4				
Σ	32	32				

Step 3: The Deviations

Now we have obtained the mean of the scores. It tells us something about the level of the participants' overall scores on the scale. The problem is that the scores also vary from the average, and we would like an index of that dispersion about the mean. As our next step, we can obtain the deviation of each score from the mean by using Equation 5.2.

Equation 5.2

$$x = X - \mu$$

where:

x is the deviation of the score X from the population mean,

X is the raw score, and

μ is the population mean of the raw scores.

The deviation is equal to the raw score minus the mean of the raw scores of X. This is placed into the deviation column (x, or X – M). That is, for each score, take the obtained value and subtract the mean. Note that roughly half of the resulting *x*s will be positive and half will be negative, and that this column will sum to zero. (If it does not, an error has been made. See Table 5.4.)

Table 5.4 Step 3 of a step-by-step approach to obtaining z-scores

Index number	Raw score	Mean	Deviation	Deviation squared	Standard deviation	*z*-score
i	X	M, $\bar{X}$	x, X–M	x^2, $(X–M)^2$	S	z
1	0	4	–4			
2	8	4	4			
3	4	4	0			
4	4	4	0			
5	8	4	4			
6	0	4	–4			
7	2	4	–2			
8	6	4	2			
Σ	32	32	0			

The Struggle Over Steps 4 and 5

In the 1920s and 1930s there was a considerable debate over whether to use average deviations or standard deviations. This provides a bit of story to help understand the logic of the z-score process, so before considering Steps 4 and 5, it is worth outlining the debate using our own example as a jumping off point.

Recall that in our last step we had eight deviations: –4, 4, 0, 0, 4, –4, –2, and 2, with a sum of 0 (see Table 5.4). There is one deviation for each participant's score. But eight deviations is a lot to think about; it would be easier to determine how much the average score deviates from the mean. The issue faced by psychometricians is how to summarize those deviations from the mean.

The obvious approach is to take the average (mean) of the eight deviations from the mean. The deviations will sum to zero, however, because the mean is their center point; if we looked at a number line, they would be balanced equally on both sides of the mean. So a simple average of the scores won't do.

One way to remedy the situation would be to take the average of the *absolute values* of the deviations, rather than taking the mean of the signed deviations (by *signed* deviations, I mean with their + and – signs). An absolute value is the numerical distance from zero (not considering negative or positive direction), meaning that all absolute values can be summed as if they were positive numbers. In simple terms, all negative numbers (as absolute values) are changed to positive numbers. The average of those absolute differences would be the average of 4, 4, 0, 0, 4, 4, 2, and 2. In this case, the average would be M = 20/8 = 2.5. Now we understand that the average score is 2.5 units from the mean. This is the *average deviation.*

Early in the 20th century, some psychometricians employed this method because it was clear, direct, and easily interpreted. In contrast, other psychometricians were unconvinced as to the merits of the case and insisted on using what initially appears to be a far less appealing approach. Let's consider the alternative.

Rather than eliminating the negative signs and taking an average of the absolute values of the deviations, the contrarians first *squared* each of the deviations. They then took the average of the squared values. That yielded a statistic they called the *variance.* The variance is the average of the *squared deviations* from the mean. The problem with this is that squared deviations are much less helpful in understanding how far each score is from the mean. To convert the squared units back to something closer to the original scores, these mathematicians then took the square root of the variance (the average of the squared deviations). That yielded an additional statistic called a *standard deviation*. The standard deviation was the square root of the average of the squared deviations from the mean.

At first glance, the psychometricians who used the average deviation ought to have prevailed because the average deviation communicates about dispersion much more directly and in the units of the original test scores. The standard deviation advocates ought to have faded away. This is not, however, what happened. Advocates of the standard deviation acknowledged that their method was not pretty, but they held an ace card in their hand: Calculate the average deviation, they observed, and it *does* nicely summarize the deviations, but what else does it get you? You couldn't calculate anything useful from it at the time. Use the variance and the standard deviation, however, and you can obtain a great variety of additional derivations and statistics—some of them quite useful.

The reason the variance and the standard deviation are used today is because of the additional statistics they lead to. For example, you can use standard deviations to calculate a new kind of language called z-scores, which became central to testing. As important, you can derive the formula for a correlation coefficient using them, which has occupied test-makers, psychologists, and other scientists since. You can't do that with the average deviation, however elegant its simplicity. The argument that the variance and standard deviation would lead to many new and powerful statistical techniques was compelling. The psychometricians who favored the *squaring the deviation* approach won the debate and most psychometricians switched to their side (e.g., McNemar, 1969, p. 20).

Now we know what we will do in Steps 4 and 5. We will calculate squared deviations, then the variance, and then the standard deviation, and leave the average deviation to today's statisticians (the average deviation is attracting renewed attention today).

Step 4: The Squared Deviations

In Step 4, the squared deviations will be calculated and entered into the table. This is simply a matter of squaring the deviations in the column marked (lower case) x, and putting the squared values (x^2) next to them. The result is shown in Table 5.5. So, if the deviation was 4 (or –4),

Table 5.5 Step 4 of a step-by-step approach to obtaining z-scores

Index number	Raw score	Mean	Deviation	Deviation squared	Standard deviation	z-score
i	X	M, $\bar{X}$	x, X–M	x^2, (X–M)^2	S	z
1	0	4	–4	16		
2	8	4	4	16		
3	4	4	0	0		
4	4	4	0	0		
5	8	4	4	16		
6	0	4	–4	16		
7	2	4	–2	4		
8	6	4	2	4		
Σ	32	32	0	72		

the squared deviation would be 16. If the deviation was 2, the squared deviation would be 4.

Step 5: The Variance and the Standard Deviation

In Step 5, we will calculate the variance and standard deviation. Thanks to our step-by-step approach, this is a nearly effortless matter. First, note that we can easily sum the squared deviations. Those deviations were the ones we just entered in the column of Table 5.5 marked x^2 or (X–M)^2. To add them up, we sum the column: that is, 16 + 16 + 0 + 0 + 16 + 16 + 4 + 4 = 72. If we divide that sum by the N (8), we obtain the variance. The formula for the variance is shown in Equation 5.3.

Equation 5.3

$$\sigma^2 = \frac{\Sigma x^2}{N}$$

where:

σ^2 is the population variance,

Σ is the operator meaning to sum up numbers,

x^2 are the squared deviations from the mean, and

N is the number of observations.

The variance is $\sigma^2 = 72/8 = 9$. In our step-by-step approach, however, the variance itself is just an intermediate step. We are actually going to use the standard deviation. The standard deviation is simply the square root of the variance. The formula for the standard deviation is shown in Equation 5.4.

Equation 5.4

$$\sigma = \sqrt{\frac{\sum x^2}{N}}$$

where:
σ is the population standard deviation,
Σ is the operator meaning to sum up numbers,
x^2 are the squared deviations from the mean, and
N is the number of observations.

To obtain the standard deviation from the variance is a simple matter, now. One simply takes the square root of the variance, or the square root of 9, which is 3. To complete this step, we place the standard deviation in each cell of the next column of the table, labeled standard deviation, as shown in Table 5.6. (You will remember from your statistics course that, for sample values, the standard deviation is biased and is typically corrected by dividing by $N-1$. We will not do that here so as to focus on the meaning of the equations.)

Table 5.6 Step 5 of a step-by-step approach to obtaining z-scores

Index number	Raw score	Mean	Deviation	Deviation squared	Standard deviation	z-score
i	X	M, $\bar{X}$	x, X–M	x^2, $(X–M)^2$	S	z
1	0	4	–4	16	3	
2	8	4	4	16	3	
3	4	4	0	0	3	
4	4	4	0	0	3	
5	8	4	4	16	3	
6	0	4	–4	16	3	
7	2	4	–2	4	3	
8	6	4	2	4	3	
Σ	32	32	0	72	24	

Step 6: The Z-Score

The z-score for the sample can now be found. The formula for the z-score is shown in Equation 5.5.

Equation 5.5

$$z = \frac{x}{\sigma} = \frac{X - \mu}{\sigma}$$

where:
z is the z-score,
x (or X – μ) represents the deviation from the population mean, and
σ is the standard deviation.

The equation tells us that the z-score equals the difference of the raw score from the mean, then divided by the standard deviation. In this example where the mean is M = 4, and the standard deviation is S = 3, test-taker seven had a score of 2, the test-taker's deviation from the mean, symbolized as x, is 2 – 4 = –2. To find the z-score, that –2 would be divided by the standard deviation. The results would be –2/3, or, in decimals, –0.67. That answer, –0.67, is the z-score. These z-scores appear in the last column of Table 5.7.

Table 5.7 Step 3 of a step-by-step approach to obtaining z-scores

Index number	Raw score	Mean	Deviation	Deviation squared	Standard deviation	z-score
i	X	M, $\bar{X}$	x, X–M	x^2, $(X–M)^2$	S	z
1	0	4	–4	16	3	–1.33
2	8	4	4	16	3	1.33
3	4	4	0	0	3	0
4	4	4	0	0	3	0
5	8	4	4	16	3	1.33
6	0	4	–4	16	3	–1.33
7	2	4	–2	4	3	–0.67
8	6	4	2	4	3	0.67

Those are the z-scores ... but how can we be sure? Z-scores are often used in further calculations. For that reason, it is a good idea to check to make sure the conversion from raw scores to z-scores has gone well. The next section explains how to do this.

When Z-Scores Are Really Z-Scores

Checking for Z-Scores

It helps to perform a brief, two-step check to ensure that the z-scores have been calculated properly. The following procedure helps ensure that the mean is zero and the standard deviation is 1. If either fails, then a mistake occurred along the way. Here is the check:

Check Step 1

Start the step-by-step process again. Treat the z-scores as raw scores and put them in the *X* column. Calculate the mean (by summing the z-scores and dividing by N) to see if it is zero. If so, you can enter *zeros* ("0") in the mean column. When you get the deviation (X – M), you will see that z-scores are their own deviations. (If the mean isn't zero, you have made a mistake.)

Check Step 2

Next, following the same steps we used to calculate the variance before, enter the squared deviations in the next column.

Check Step 3

The last step is to find the variance of the z-scores. For that, sum the squared deviations. They happen to sum to 7.974, which is approximately equal to 8, and yields a variance very close to 1.0 (actually, 0.9968). Why not 8? Well, the z-scores were recorded only to the hundredths place in this example, and that rounding error accounts for the discrepancy. Nonetheless, a 0.99 is fairly close to 1.00, and acceptable in this instance. If the variance is approximately 1.00, then the standard deviation will be

Table 5.8 Step 1 of a step-by-step check of the z-scores

Index number	Raw score	Mean	Deviation	Deviation squared
i	X	M, $\bar{X}$	x, X–M	x^2, $(X–M)^2$
1	–1.33	0	–1.33	1.769
2	1.33	0	1.33	1.769
3	0	0	0	0
4	0	0	0	0
5	1.33	0	1.33	1.769
6	–1.33	0	–1.33	1.769
7	–0.67	0	–0.67	0.449
8	0.67	0	0.67	0.449
Σ	0	0	0	7.974

approximately 1.00 as well, because the square root of 1.00 is 1.00. These scores have a mean of 0 and a standard deviation of (approximately) 1.0. They have passed the test as z-scores.

The Properties of Z-Scores Reviewed

Z-scores are a universal language, because once a test is converted to z-scores, the test scores have a mean that is equal to zero and a standard deviation equal to 1.0. Almost all mental scales can be converted meaningfully into the common language of z-scores.

Some of the mysteries of tests have been explained here. Test scores are often reported in ways meant to be helpful to test-takers: as positive, whole numbers. Behind the scenes, however, most test scores are computed as z-scores—a universal language based on a comparison of each person's test performance in relation to the average of the group. In Chapter 6, I will examine how z-scores are converted back into the scales that are reported to test-takers.

In the next chapters, the idea of the z-score will be more fully developed. The concept of the z-score will be employed to better understand the idea of norming and scaling a test. The z-score also will be used as the basis for calculating a statistic called the *correlation*, which indicates the relationship between two variables, such as between a test and a real-life criterion.

CHAPTER 6

Comparing Test Scores

Interpreting the Level of a Test Score

When a teacher passes back a graded assignment to the students, a lot goes on in the classroom. Some students quickly glance at their test scores, taking care to prevent others from looking at them. A few students suppress a fleeting expression of pleasure on their faces. Most students regard it as polite, or at least prudent, to hide any reactions to a high grade. Other students exhale in relief. Still other students maintain a poker face that reveals absolutely nothing about how they have done. Some students make a point of not looking, and not caring.

For students who do care about their grades and their performance in school, the first few moments of reaction may be only the beginning. Many students become casual detectives at that point, and a small investigation may unfold: "How did you do?" they whisper to a trusted friend. "I'll tell you my score if you tell me yours" or "See if you can find out how Sophie did."

Some teachers downplay the importance of this comparison: "All that matters is your own grade," they say, or "Don't get too hung up on the grade." More officially, some educators and psychologists speak of *competence-based testing*. That is, so long as the student meets a basic level of competence in an area, she or he has done what is necessary and any further comparisons are superfluous. Other educators, however, hope to inspire students to attain higher levels of accomplishments.

For the achievement-oriented student, or the student interested in accurate self-knowledge, simply knowing he has met a standard of competence is insufficient. For a student with a test score in hand, knowing how his friends have performed represents something more significant than idle chatter; it represents an intuitive appreciation of the need for score comparisons to interpret how they have done. The comparisons are often sophisticated. On a 100-point test, the friend who typically earns a high A is expected to have a score in the middle 90s or better. If he received only an 89, that could be good news, because it might indicate that the test was unusually hard, and that even the brainiest students failed to break the 90-percent level. In such a case, the teacher might decide to adjust the scores so that more people got an A. Even if the teacher does not curve the particular test, a score of 85 seems—and is—a bit better by comparison.

The achieving student possesses an intuitive understanding that comparative level matters. In the world of school, careers, and even relationships, people are rank ordered and these classifications may have consequences. Moms, dads, and friends can rejoice that just about everyone is good at something: honesty, caring, intelligence, courage, and creativity are just a few areas in which someone might excel. Still, each attribute carries its own promise, and knowing one's relative standing is important to some people.

The exact scores awarded by a teacher on a classroom test require a secondary interpretation: How did the A students do? How did the average students do? How did the lower achievers do? This question becomes all the more important as tests become more important. Scores from IQ tests, tests of psychopathology such as the Minnesota Multiphasic Personality Inventory (MMPI), and other tests become meaningful only when compared with the scores of other people.

What Are Test Norms?

Criterion-Referenced Tests

Tests can be criterion-referenced or norm-referenced, and both types have their applications. *Criterion-referenced tests* have an agreed-upon standard of good performance called the criterion. Criterion-referenced tests are designed to indicate whether or not a person has mastered a specific basic skill.

An example of a criterion-referenced test is the written driver's license exam. Scores on the driver's license test must meet required standards, such as that 85 percent of the items should be correct. Comparisons to other people's scores hardly matter; rather, those who administer the test want to ensure that everyone drives safely: You simply must know what a stop sign is and what side of the road to drive on.

The criterion-referenced technique is less clearly applied when a person's capacity to engage in complex reasoning is measured. For example, there may be no clear criterion for solving complex mathematics problems (where there is often more than one way to solve a problem). Equally, it is difficult to specify a criterion for a high level of the need for achievement. How much is too little, enough, or too much? The answer to that often will depend upon the person and her goals.

Norm-Referenced Tests

Norm-referenced tests are based on how people perform in comparison to the average—also known as the norm. For areas of testing in which exceeding a basic level of competence is desirable, people's attributes are compared to one another, and the higher a person scores on an attribute relative to others, the higher her score. In norm-referenced testing, an individual's test score is compared to the scores of other test-takers. Recall that z-scores (Chapter 5) compare people's test scores to one another; they form a basis for norm-referenced testing.

The Purpose of Norming a Test

Is a person's test score high, low, or somewhere in the middle? The purpose of *norming* test scores is to better understand how high or low an individual's test score is. To norm a test means to collect test scores from a large sample of individuals and then to compare the score of a new test-taker to the original group's performance.

If the new test-taker's score is near the average of the original group, the test-taker's level is viewed as about average. If the test-taker's score is above the average of the original group, then the test-taker's level is viewed as above average, and if the test-taker's score is below the average of the original group, then the level is viewed as below average. Put another way, the meaning of the individual's score is enhanced by comparing it to an understandable criterion—the performance of similar individuals.

The key issue becomes one of relative standing in a group—and the nature of that group. In particular, some groups allow for comparisons better than others.

Issues Concerning Standardization and Comparison Samples

Standardization Samples

Major tests have *standardization samples* associated with them. A standardization sample is a large sample of individuals with whom future test-takers are to be compared. The test results for the standardization sample—the mean and standard deviations, for example—are referred to as the *test norms.*

The Size of the Standardization Sample

A test's standardization sample must be sizeable enough to convey good information. If the sample is too small, even if it is randomly sampled, it may not provide a good representation of the population of interest. The larger and more representative the standardization sample is, the more assurance there is that the test average and other benchmarks will be good indicators of typical test performance. The estimate of the mean improves as the number of participants, symbolized by N, increases. An ideal sample size for a standardization sample is N = 1,000 or more.

Representative Standardization Samples

The test-taker's score is typically most informative when it is compared to the scores of similar people who have taken the test under comparable conditions. For example, a high school junior's overall knowledge of algebra would be reasonably compared to the scores of other high school juniors. If the student's score is among the highest, relative to a large group of other high school juniors, then the student's score can be considered an indicator of very high performance. On the other hand, if the junior scores higher than 30 other second-grade children who took the same test, the comparison is less informative, because second graders simply cannot be compared to high school juniors with regard to their knowledge of algebra.

The point is to select a representative and meaningful sample of other individuals for comparison. To some extent, the choice of a comparison group must involve common sense. A highly gifted high school junior might choose to compare her algebra levels against college students, or even graduate students in mathematics. Such comparisons would be unusual, but meaningful in the case of such a gifted individual.

For the most part, however, one's qualities are best compared against those of one's peers. The extraversion of a 22-year-old adult is best compared against the extraversion of other adults of about the same age. A middle manager's achievement motive—her desire to excel at work—is best compared to the achievement motive of other middle managers who have been tested in other similar companies.

Comparison Groups

The process of obtaining a standardization sample can be challenging, time consuming, and expensive. For that reason, many smaller tests in use don't have formal standardization samples. In the place of such samples, the test authors may report scores from smaller groups called comparison groups. *Comparison groups* are groups of participants, often a few hundred in size, to whom the test has been given and for which statistics such as means and standard deviations have been reported. Some tests have both an overall standardization sample and comparison samples. The algebra test discussed earlier might report data from all high school students, as well as special statistics reported for comparison groups such as high school students with impaired hearing.

The Lighter Side of Norm

Some psychologists have seen a humorous side to the work involved in collecting test norms. Glenn Ellenbogen (1980/1986) reported the construction of a new psychometric measure, the Scale of Mental Abilities Requiring Thinking Somewhat (S.M.A.R.T.S.). His report appeared in the *Journal of Polymorphous Perversity*—a satirical journal named after Freud's term for the idea that people can obtain pleasure from various parts of their bodies. The article's section on *Norms* began: "Our subject, Norman (or Norm, as he preferred to be called), was a freshman at New York University." Ellenbogen continued:

> After carefully weighing the possible threats to internal and external validity, as well as to job security, we decided to administer the S.M.A.R.T.S. test to Norm many, many times in order that we would end up with enough numbers, data, and statistics to construct at least one table. The scores, then, presented in Table 1, are really Norm's. (Ellenbogen 1980/1986, p. 102)

Test Scores and the Bell-Shaped Curve

As a test is administered to more and more people, the distribution of the test scores becomes better known. The distribution of test scores refers to the relative number of times each test score will occur in a given sample. For example, Figure 6.1 shows a score distribution of four possible scores on a test, 1, 2, 3, and 4, that occur about equally—that is, 25 percent of the test-takers get a 1, 25 percent get a 2, 25 percent get a 3, and 25 percent get a 4. We can say, "Oh, a test score of '4'—that puts you in the top 25 percent of all test-takers on that feature."

This brings us to a curiosity of mental life: Many mental qualities are distributed in the form of a bell-shaped curve. This curve also goes by the name of the normal distribution. If the above four scores were to follow the bell curve, the distribution of scores would look like the result shown

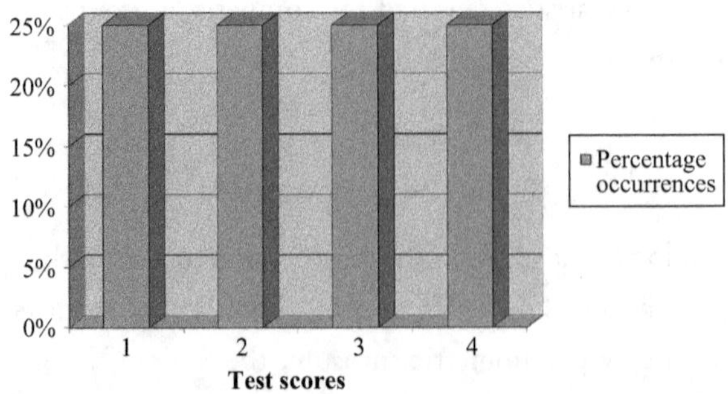

Figure 6.1 A distribution of test scores for four outcomes of equal probability

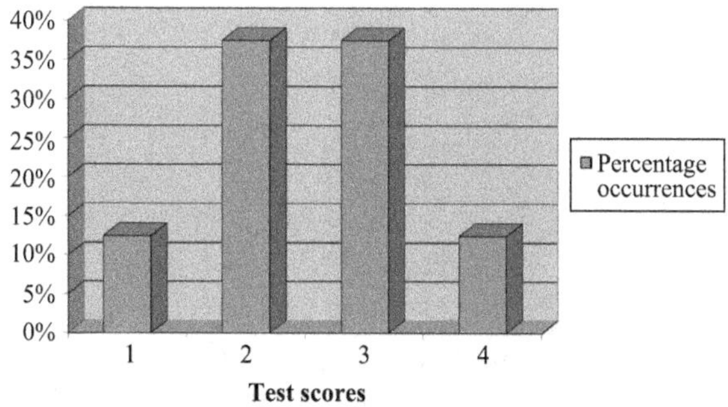

Figure 6.2 A bell-shaped distribution of test scores for four outcomes

in Figure 6.2. Notice that the score bars in Figure 6.1 have taken on different lengths in Figure 6.2, with the outer bars (representing scores of 1 and 4) shorter than the middle bars. The overall figure becomes more bell-shaped as we add more scores (look ahead to Figure 6.6 for an example).

The technical name for the frequency distribution in Figure 6.2 is the *binomial distribution.* The binomial distribution often approximates the distribution of test scores for large numbers of people; it generates percentages for the range of scores, which, when graphed, resemble a bell-shaped curve.

Appreciating the Binomial Distribution

A reasonable question is to ask is "*Why* are test scores distributed in a bell-shaped form?"

To answer this question, let's turn to a mathematical pattern known as *Pascal's triangle.* This pattern was first described by the Chinese mathematician Yang Hui and later discussed in detail by Blaise Pascal (Conway & Guy, 1996; Pickover, 2001).

The triangle is created with a 1 at the top and additional rows below. The first 10 rows are shown in Figure 6.3. Can you see the pattern?

If we look at a row of Pascal's triangle (and we always know the top row has a single 1 in it), we can always calculate the next row. Notice that each row begins and ends with a 1. We can use one simple rule to generate the whole triangle; to use the rule, however, you must imagine that there are 0s at the start and end of every row. Under that condition, the triangle

```
                          1
                       1     1
                    1     2     1
                 1     3     3     1
              1     4     6     4     1
           1     5    10    10     5     1
        1     6    15    20    15     6     1
     1     7    21    35    35    21     7     1
  1     8    28    56    70    56    28     8     1
1    9    36    84   126   126    84    36     9    1
                         ...
```

Figure 6.3 Pascal's triangle

begins with a 1 at the top and thereafter, every number in the triangle that follows is the sum of the two numbers above it. In row 2, the 1 on the left is the sum of the upper left zero (not shown) and the 1 at the top of the triangle. The 1 on the right of row 2 is a sum of the 1 at the top and the 0 to its right (also not shown).

Now look at the fifth row as a further example. Once again, the outer 1s are the sum of the zeros (not shown) and 1s above them. That row's middle three numbers are 4, 6, and 4. Each of the middle three numbers is a sum of the two numbers above it: 4 (1 + 3 above it), 6 (3 + 3), and 4 (3 + 1).

What Does Pascal's Triangle Tell Us About Mental Features?

Pascal's triangle corresponds to a real-world phenomenon: It helps to envision a rather odd machine to fully appreciate this idea. The machine is called a *Galton Machine* because the English mathematician Charles Galton built the first one and used it in public lectures about statistics. Galton referred to the machine as a *quincunx*, and it also is known by that name. I first saw the machine years ago in a movie in which white-coated scientists had built a frame in the shape of a triangle with pegs inside and a short opening tube on top. In Figure 6.4, I have placed Pascal's triangle next to a sketch of how the pegs were positioned (which is on the right).

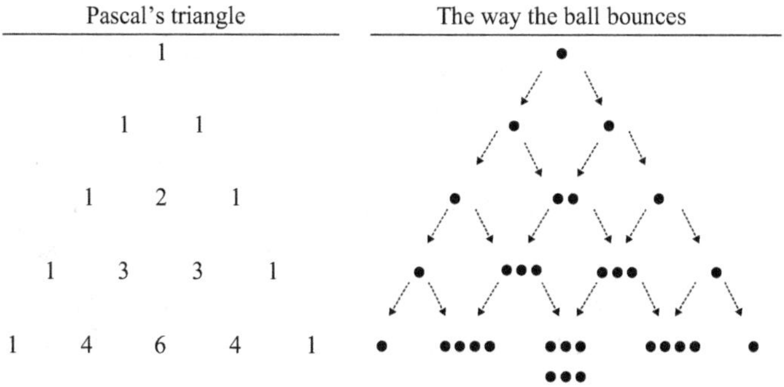

Figure 6.4 Pascal's triangle (left) and following the bouncing balls through the triangle (right)

The scientists dropped balls through a vertical tube, which emptied into the top of the triangle. The balls would hit pegs arranged in the triangular area. Each time a ball hit a peg, it would continue to fall downward either to the right or the left side of the peg (the encasement ensured that the ball would not jump away from the pegs), and then hit pegs on the next row down.

There was a 50 percent chance a ball would go to either side of a given peg. The pegs were placed in the same positions as the numbers in Pascal's triangle. As it turns out, Pascal's triangle predicts the exact likelihood that a ball would land in any given position. More balls will end up at the middle of the base of the triangle, while few end up at the extreme ends of the base. This phenomenon is represented by the higher numbers at the center of Pascal's triangle. Galton's machine, the quincunx, brings the physics of Pascal's triangle to life.

Imagine a ball dropping through the triangle. When it is at position 1, at the top of the triangle, it has a 100 percent likelihood of being in that spot. From row 1 to row 2, it can move either to the right or the left. If everything is random, the likelihood it would move down to the right is 1/2 (50 percent), and the likelihood it would move down to the left is also 1/2 (50 percent). From row 2 to row 3, let's first follow up on the 50 percent likelihood the ball moved to the left.

At the left side of the third row, the odds the ball will land toward the outside left will be 1/4 (25 percent); the same is true of moving to the middle. Had the ball bounced from row 2 to the *right* of row 3, it would similarly exhibit odds of landing on the outside right of 1/4 (25 percent), and have the same probability of moving to the middle. As many balls descend from row 2 to row 3 through the triangle, they will have twice the odds of moving toward the middle than to the outside positions, because balls will move there from either side. The odds of moving toward the middle for any single ball in row 3 are 1/4 + 1/4 = 1/2, or 50 percent.

Pascal's triangle tells us the odds that the ball will fall in a particular place in the row of a triangle. To calculate the odds, first identify the number in the given position of a row of the triangle, and divide the number by the sum of the entries in a row to obtain the probability. So, row 1 is 1/1 = 100 percent. There is a 100 percent chance the ball will start there. Row 2 is 1/2 and 1/2, or a 50 percent chance that the ball will pass through the right spot, and 50 percent chance it will pass to the left. Row 3 goes 1/4, 2/4, and 1/4.

What we are describing here is a mathematical world in which an outcome (the ball's movement) is subject to a series of chances that each has an equal likelihood of occurring (50 percent). As the number of possible outcomes increases, the final distribution looks more like a bell curve.

To draw an analogy between the triangle and test scores, consider the five numbers in row 5 of Figure 6.4: The entries in the row are 1, 4, 6, 4, and 1. Each position from left to right can represent a total score on a five-item dichotomous scale of extraversion (that is, five yes or no questions of the sort, "I am outgoing"). In this example, a *no* would be given a value of *0* and a *yes* would be given a value of *1*. The total score would range from a low of 0 (five no responses) to a high of 5 (five yes responses). Now imagine a ball is dropped from the top. The ball's position is analogous to the test-taker's score. When the ball falls to the right (a *yes*), it means that the individual's extraversion test score is higher; any time it moves to the left (a *no*), it represents the test-taker's extraversion response is lower.

The influences on a person's mental test score can be thought of as the forces that move the ball to the right or left. Each time the test score (ball) moves to the right, it may be pushed by a different influence. The ball (the test score) might move to the right if the individual has inherited a particular gene for social affection, and do so again if the individual inherited a gene for lively emotions (a feature of extraversion). The ball might move to the right again if the individual experienced sociable surroundings as an infant, and yet again if the adult has learned that sociability carries rewards with it (e.g., a promotion in a sales position). As the influences add up, the ball (the test score) moves toward the right.

For a person to encounter either none or all of the influences associated with extraversion would be very unlikely. Correspondingly, it would be unlikely for the ball to settle all the way to the left or all the way to the right. What is most common would be to have only some of these influences for extraversion. That is represented by the fact that the ball is more likely to land toward the middle, representing one of the intermediate scores.

Comparing the Triangle to a Test Score Distribution

The triangle can be related to the binomial distribution as follows. For our purposes, the top of the triangle can be thought of as containing a test that yields just one score. The second row has two scores (two outcomes, e.g., one dichotomous item), the third row depicts a test with three scores (three outcomes), and so forth.

As I suggested above, if each number in the triangle is divided by the total sum of the row, that provides the likelihood that a given outcome will occur, assuming events take place according to the binomial distribution. I have illustrated this in the modified triangle shown in Figure 6.5 (cf., Conway & Guy, 1996).

In the last row shown, if we do the division, the percentages equal (approximately) 1.6, 9.4, 23.4, 31.3, 23.4, 9.4, and 1.6 percent. As more rows are added, the distribution becomes smoother, until the figure approximates what we have come to call the bell curve. A version of the bar graph representing the percents from the last row of Figure 6.5 is shown in Figure 6.6, where the bars have begun to take on the shape of a curve.

The binomial distribution (as indicated by Pascal's triangle) gradually approaches a perfect bell curve as more rows are added and the graphical depiction I have illustrated is continued. I will describe the relationship between the binomial and the normal curve next. The bell curve it generates is closely approximated by the normal distribution.

1/1

1/2 1/2

1/4 2/4 1/4

1/8 3/8 3/8 1/8

1/16 4/16 6/16 4/16 1/16

1/32 5/32 10/32 10/32 5/32 1/32

1/64 6/64 15/64 20/64 15/64 6/64 1/64

Figure 6.5 Pascal's triangle as a probability distribution

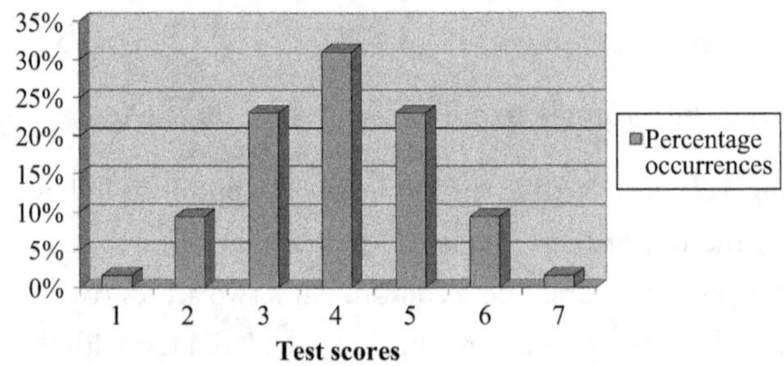

Figure 6.6 An example of a binomially-distributed set of test scores, with seven possible levels

Tricks With Z-Scores: The Normal Distribution and Percentiles

The Normal Distribution, the Unit Normal Distribution, and Percentiles

The bell curve is often also equated to the normal distribution—also known as the *normal curve*. The normal distribution is a frequency histogram (commonly called a bar graph) in the shape of a curve that closely approximates the binomial distribution as the intervals become increasingly numerous. In fact, there is no such thing in nature as a normal curve or a normal distribution; what really exists is the binomial distribution. The normal distribution is a mathematical model intended to approximate the binomial distribution. The normal curve allows us to make calculations about the binomial distribution rather quickly and conveniently.

If we have test scores that are roughly normally distributed (that is, distributed according to the binomial distribution), the normal distribution readily allows us the opportunity to understand the qualities of a given set of test scores.

From here forward, I will discuss only the normal-curve approximation, leaving behind the binomial distribution that we have explored. Remember that the normal curve approximates the binomial distribution when we are dealing with a large number of possible tests scores and observations.

The Unit Normal Distribution

A normal curve of z-scores has a special name, the *unit normal distribution*. This is the normal distribution that corresponds to a set of z-scores: any distribution of scores with a mean of 0 and standard deviation of 1. It is known by this term because the standard deviation of the z-scores equals one unit, or 1.

Back to the Z-Score

As we saw in the last chapter, a set of raw test scores can be converted into z-scores. Such a conversion ensures that the scores have a mean of 0 and a standard deviation of 1.0. By applying the z-score transformation outlined in the previous chapter, we accomplished a number of things. The procedure stripped away many of the non-essential aspects of the given test that was administered; one of those is the test's average score. Why is the average score nonessential? Remember that a test's mean will be substantially dependent upon what kinds of items are on the test and how many items there are (see Chapter 3 for more about test items). For example, if a Likert scale is being used, the mean is dependent on whether the response alternatives are on a 3-, 7-, or 21-point scale.

Let's say a test-maker wants to measure extraversion. She may have proposed a statement such as "I like parties" and then followed it with a 4-point scale: "Agree 1 2 3 4 Disagree." Another test-maker might have used the same question with a 7-point scale: "Agree 1 2 3 4 5 6 7 Disagree." Still another test-maker might have doubled the number of similar test items because lengthening the test might improve it.

Each such decision changes the range of possible scores on the test. The possible scores a person could attain might range from 10 to 40 for a 10-item test with a 4-point response scale, or from 20 to 80 for a test double the length. The variety of possible scales (and number of items) that could be used complicates how to interpret the magnitude of the test scores.

The z-score process ensures that the effects on the test mean resulting from the chosen response scale and the number of items on the test are stripped away. The remaining significant information is the person's rank on the attribute being measured (e.g., extraversion). Scores from all tests are now plotted on an idealized z-score scale in which the mean = 0, the standard deviation = 1.

This conversion of test scores into z-scores preserves everyone's standing relative to one another. The person with the highest test score still has the highest score, the person with the lowest test score still has the lowest, and the person in the middle is, indeed, still in the middle.

At this point, we can conclude some things about normally distributed z-scores. As always, the mean is 0. But now we can add that—if the scores are normally distributed—about 68 percent of the scores fall between a z-score of –1 and +1. About 95 percent of the scores fall between z-scores of –2 and +2 (more precisely, ±1.96). Finally, about 99.7 percent of the scores fall between z-scores of –3 and +3.

The position of a given z-score in relation to the rest of the distribution is shown in Figure 6.7.

The area under a portion of the curve represents the likelihood that a score will be in that interval. Consider the area from –4.0 to 0. That covers just about 50 percent of the curve, and, indeed, half the area of the curve is below 0. The other 50 percent is above 0.

This relationship between z-scores and probabilities of a score allows us to assign percentage ranks to people who score along the normal distribution. Typically, a z-score of –2.33 is roughly equal to the 1st percentile. A z-score of –.84 would mark something close to the 20th percentile, 0 the 50th percentile, .84 the 80th percentile, and so on. Some further

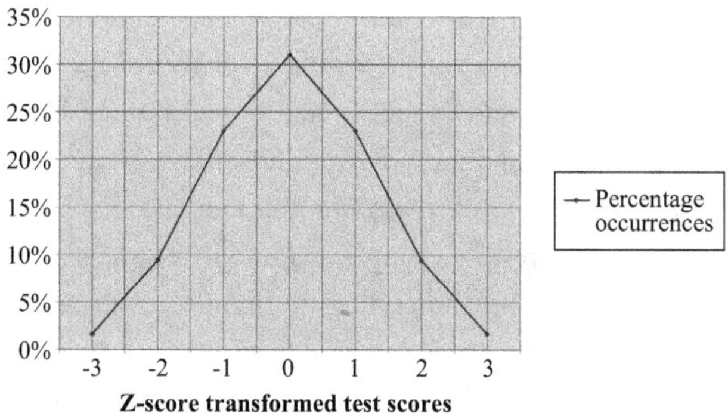

Figure 6.7 A depiction of the unit normal distribution

Table 6.1 Conversion table of z-scores and approximate percentiles

z-score	Approximate percentile
2.33 or greater	99th or higher
1.28	90th
.84	80th
.52	70th
.25	60th
.00	50th
−.25	40th
−.52	30th
−.84	20th
−1.28	10th
less than −2.33	lower than 1st

relationships are illustrated in Table 6.1. More complete z-tables, which convert from z-scores to percentages (and back again), can be found as the first appendix in most statistics books, as well as on the web.

Scaling and the Z-Score

The z-score is a dream come true for a mathematician. It is not, however, for the test-taker. Test takers—those who must deal with their own scores—understandably don't want to know they received a .0875 or a 1.897 on a test, let alone a −.14. A z-score of −.14 is just slightly below average; however, because it is negative it will seem like a poor score to many test-takers.

It is for that reason that z-scores are put on another more easily interpreted scale for test-takers. This new scale is often used because it has a specific standard deviation and mean, both of which make it (relatively) easy to communicate and discuss. For this reason, I will refer to it here as the *communicated scale*. Once the communicated scale has been chosen, converting from z-scores is as simple as multiplying the z-score by the desired standard deviation and adding in the new scale's desired mean. This transformation can be made using Equation 6.1.

There are a number of commonly communicated scales one can choose from including IQ scales, T-scales, and SAT scales. Let's look at each of them in turn.

Equation 6.1

$$C = (z * \sigma_c) + \mu_c$$

where:
C is the communicated scale: the scale presented to the test-taker and the test-user,
z is the z-score of the original raw score,
σ_C is the standard deviation of the new, communicated scale, and
μ_C is the mean of the communicated scale.

The IQ Scale

IQ scores have a mean (μ) of 100 and a standard deviation (σ) of 15. Converting a z-score to the IQ scale simply involves multiplying the z by 15 and then adding 100. Here is an example:

- A z-score of 1.0 would be multiplied by 15 (the standard deviation), and then 100 (the mean) would be added, to get an IQ of 115.
- A z-score of –.5 would be multiplied by 15 to get –7.5, and then the mean would be added to get 92.5.

The T-Scale

T-Scales are set up with a mean of 50 and a standard deviation of 10. A variety of tests are scored in this way. Probably the best known of these tests is the MMPI; it has 10 clinical scales, each of which measures a form of psychopathology such as schizophrenia, hysteria, or psychopathic deviancy. For example:

- To convert a z-score of −1.5 to a T-Scale would require simply multiplying −1.5 by the standard deviation of 10, to obtain −15, and then adding 50, yielding a score of 35.

The SAT Scale

Let's say we want to convert a set of z-scores to the kind of scale used by the College Board's SAT test. The SAT is designed to have a mean of 500 and a standard deviation of 100. You may notice that the psychometricians at the College Board used the T-Scale described earlier (M = 50, S = 10) and multiplied both the mean and the standard deviation by 10 to get the SAT scale.

To convert a z-score to an SAT score, we once again apply the steps of Equation 6.1:

- A z-score of 0 (the mean) would be multiplied by 100 (yielding 0), and then 500 would be added, to obtain an SAT score of 500.
- A z-score of −1 would be multiplied by 100 (yielding −100), and then 500 would be added, to obtain an SAT score of 400.
- A z-score of 2.34 would be multiplied by 100 (yielding 234), and then 500 would be added, to obtain an SAT of 735.

In actuality, the distribution of scores on the SAT vary somewhat from year to year, and the organization that authors the test, ETS, has allowed the test mean to drift from 500 at times.

Normalizing the Test

Sometimes a test is not normally (binomially) distributed, but rather deviates from the idealized form by a noticeable degree. A common deviation from the normal curve occurs when the distribution of scores is *skewed.* This term refers to the fact that the scores are mostly dispersed at the high or low end of the distribution. The test-maker, however, may want to scale the scores as if the test is normally distributed, which can be done by shifting the scores along the normal curve so that the proportion of scores needed (the specific proportion as dictated by the normal curve) is found within each interval. Normalization, for example, is a property of many T-Scales. Guilford and Fruchter (1973, pp. 468–474) provide detailed instructions for performing this transformation in the context of T-Scales.

A Note on Skipping the Z-Score Process

It is not always necessary to convert to z-scores to norm a test. Test norms can be quite informal, as often occurs in a school classroom.

For example, if a teacher wants to rank students on an exam, the students who took the exam will constitute a good sample. The teacher knows that, for the students to be in her class, they were pre-selected as appropriate to the particular school. After years in the classroom, the instructor may have a feel for how students ought to perform on the exam. This intuition allows her to scale the test without standardization or computations of deviations from the mean. So, the teacher can assign some As, Bs, and Cs in a customary fashion with some confidence. Although z-scores won't typically come into play here, the principle of comparing a student's test scores to norms is the same: The teacher has informal norms from having taught a course a number of times, so that she can recognize an unusually good or unusually low performing group of students, and adjust the grades accordingly.

In other forms of mental testing, however, the test administrator may not have past experience with the test or knowledge of local norms. In these situations, a larger sample could be useful.

Revisiting the Importance of the Sample Size

If an assessor will be making important determinations about a person, then using a test that has undergone formal standardization is desirable. Remember that sample size is denoted by the symbol *N*. Very small samples (small *N*s) do not tell us very much about a test's mean. Using large samples increases our confidence in what a test score indicates.

Say we administer a new test to a sample of nine people and obtain a mean of 140, with a standard deviation of 20. Under such circumstances, the best we could say is that the actual test mean falls (19 out of 20 times) between roughly 127 and 153—an imprecise estimate, if we would like to know how an individual performed in relation to others.

On the other hand, say that we administer a new test to a sample of 1,600 people, obtaining the same mean of 140 and standard deviation of 20. The much larger sample size allows us to say that the actual mean falls (19 out of 20 times) between roughly 139 and 141—a fairly narrow range, which provides adequate accuracy for most purposes (Guilford & Fruchter, 1973, p. 131).

The Broader Meaning of the Test Score

This chapter has explored just one aspect of a test score: its meaning relative to other individuals' scores on the same dimension. There is more to the meaning of a test score than how high or low a person scores, however. To establish that broader meaning, it is useful to compare and contrast people's scores with other variables of interest. To do this requires relating the test scores to other variables using a statistic you are already likely to be familiar with, called the *correlation coefficient*. The next chapter will explore how to calculate and interpret correlations using z-scores. By doing so, we will gradually build our skills at interpreting test scores—a process that will continue through the chapters on reliability and validity.

CHAPTER 7
Correlating Test Scores

Test Scores: Can You Relate?

A person's first question after taking a test is often "How well did I do?" That question can be answered by comparing the individual's score to the scores of other test-takers. Knowing a person's score in relation to other people, however, is not very helpful unless one knows what the score *means.*

Ultimately, we want to understand what the test scores obtained by test-takers mean. In the case of an intelligence test, for example, we want to know whether or not the test scores really indicate a person's ability to solve problems well.

The most crucial debates that arise in the testing field concern what a given test *really* measures. I might claim to have written a new measure of intelligence, but what do I mean by intelligence? How can I be sure the test really does measure this attribute? Throughout this book, I have casually mentioned that a specific test may measure intelligence, extraversion, or friendliness. Can we really know what is being measured?

This question ultimately relates to a test's *validity*, and is crucial (Chapter 11 is about test validity).

To begin to answer the question, we must be able to quantify the relationship between two variables. For example, we may wish to quantify the relationship between a new intelligence test that has up-to-date language and content and an existing older test in which researchers have considerable confidence. This will go some way toward determining what the new test measures: If scores on the new intelligence test are highly similar to scores on the older well-accepted measure, then researchers may have some justifiable confidence in the new test. However, if the new intelligence test bears little or no relationship to that pre-existing test, the maker of the new test may have to justify the discrepancy.

The Meaning of the Correlation Coefficient

What Does a Correlation Coefficient Do?

There are statistics that summarize how closely two variables relate to each other. One widely used index that allows for the comparison of two variables is called the Pearson product-moment correlation coefficient, or simply, the correlation coefficient. This is an index that describes the degree of association between two variables.

General Properties of the Correlation Coefficient

The correlation coefficient ranges from –1.0 to 1.0. A correlation of 1.0 represents a perfect positive relationship; a correlation of –1.0 represents a perfect negative relationship, and a correlation of zero indicates no relationship.

Positive correlations occur when two variables go up and down together, such that if the first variable is high, so is the second variable, and when the first variable is low, so is the second variable. Some examples of positive correlations are the relations between height and weight, years of education and income, and liveliness and sociability. If the relationship between the two variables is perfect, such that a rise in the first variable is always reflected in a proportional rise in the second variable, then the correlation between the two variables is $r = 1.0$, where r indicates the correlation. However, the relationship is usually less than perfect; in such a case, the correlation takes on a value between $r = 0$ and 1.0.

Negative correlations occur when the two variables under consideration move in opposite directions, such that when the first variable is high, the second variable is low, and when the first is low, the second is high. In these cases, the variables are said to have a negative or inverse relationship. Negative correlations range from –1.0 to 0. If it is a perfectly proportional negative relationship, then $r = -1.0$. If the relationship is less than perfectly negative (the most common circumstance), then the correlation will be between $r = -1.0$ and 0. Examples of negative correlations are found between years of education and years spent in jail, as well as the price of a car and its age.

Finally, if there is no relationship between the variables, such that when one variable is high or low, it says nothing about the status of the other, then the correlation is said to be zero. An example of a correlation likely to be close to zero would be the price of ice cream in Rome, Italy, and the average height of police officers in Burlington, Vermont, measured annually from 1990 to 1999.

The Origins of the Correlation Coefficient

Mathematicians developed the correlation coefficient so as to assess the relationship between two variables. The 19th-century mathematician and psychologist, Sir Francis Galton, and his student, Sir Karl Pearson, were centrally involved in this. Like many British scientists of the time, they were very interested in heredity and, in particular, in quantifying the strength of relationships between parents and their offspring for various qualities.

In one series of studies, Galton grew sweet peas into mature plants, weighed the seeds, planted them, and then examined the seeds of the daughter plants. He graphed the mother seed weight to the daughter seed weight in a scatterplot to see the relationship. In other studies, he graphed (human) fathers' heights in a scatterplot and compared them to the heights of their sons. By graphing these relationships, Galton could see that some relationships between parent and child were very strong, while others were relatively weak (Stanton, 2001).

Galton's graphs represented a first step toward the development of a correlation coefficient. As such, it is worth looking at a specific example: Table 7.1 presents the z-scores of seven people who took two tests, X and Y.

To create a scatterplot of two variables, a chart is created with two lines that are perpendicular to each other. The horizontal line is called the *X axis*. The vertical line is the *Y axis*. Intervals are often placed along both axes. If the scatterplot concerns paired sets of z-scores, as in Table 7.1, these intervals will divide the range from about –3.0 to 3.0, because most z-scores fall within that range.

Next, points are *plotted*—positioned—in the space defined by the two axes. To do this, a specific pair of observations is selected—for example,

Table 7.1 Pairs of z-scores generated by tests X and Y

i	z_X	z_Y
1	−2.7	−2.8
2	0.5	1.0
3	−2.0	−2.3
4	2.0	1.5
5	1.5	3.0
6	2.5	2.7
7	−1.0	−0.5
...	...	...

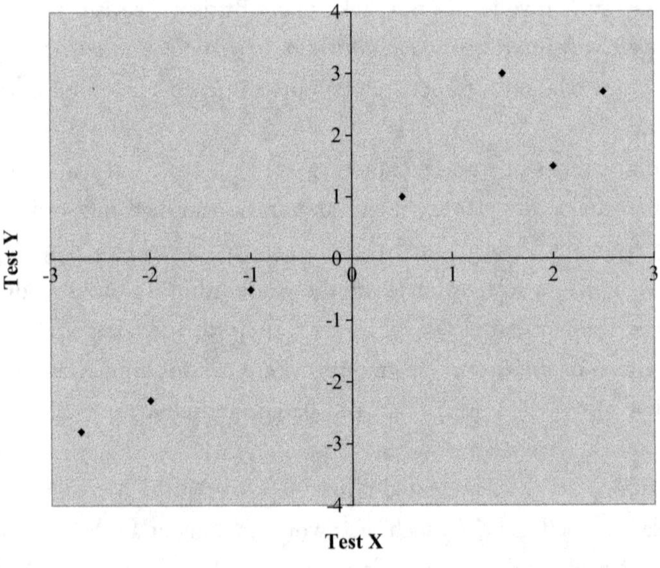

Figure 7.1 A scatterplot of z-scores on tests X and Y

the first person's score on tests X and Y: −2.7, and −2.8 (from Table 7.1). Those paired scores are then plotted in the graph. For example, the particular point −2.7, −2.8 is at the bottom left of the scatterplot. This process then is continued for each of the remaining pairs of points. The scatterplot shown in Figure 7.1 illustrates the first seven pairs of points of Table 7.1.

Galton asked Pearson to develop a statistic that would summarize that sort of relationship. Starting with such an idea, Pearson then tried to work out something useful and elegant. It would be elegant, for example, if the index of association between the two variables would vary between some sensible boundaries (such as −1.0 and 1.0).

Explaining the Correlation Coefficient

Computational versus Conceptual Equations

When I first learned the correlation coefficient, an instructor showed me (what I regarded as) an intimidating formula for its computation. I have reproduced it in Equation 7.1. You may have seen something like it in your statistics course. The formula appears complex in part because it is a *computational equation.* Computational versions of equations have been optimized to make it easy to calculate answers by hand with large numbers of observations. This formula for the correlation serves its purpose, but it is nearly impossible to understand, unless one has a moderate degree of familiarity with statistical expressions.

Equation 7.1

$$r_{XY} = \frac{\Sigma XY - \frac{\Sigma X \Sigma Y}{N}}{\sqrt{\left(\Sigma X^2 - \frac{(\Sigma X)^2}{N}\right)\left(\Sigma Y - \frac{(\Sigma Y)^2}{N}\right)}}$$

where:

r_{XY} is the correlation coefficient between scores on tests X and Y,
X is the raw score on test X,
Y is the raw score on test Y, and
N is the number of paired observations.

I am not going to use the computational formula beyond showing it as Equation 7.1. Now that statistical software is available to compute most problems involving large sets of numbers, there is little need to teach this equation, except to satisfy historical curiosity. There are more meaningful and easier formulae to use. A *conceptual* equation for the correlation coefficient similar to what Karl Pearson developed is reproduced here as Equation 7.2. This version of the equation, which is algebraically equivalent to Equation 7.1, reduces the correlation to its statistical essentials.

Equation 7.2

$$r_{XY} = \frac{\sum z_x z_y}{N}$$

where:
r_{XY} is the correlation coefficient between scores on tests X and Y,
z_X is a z-score on test X,
z_Y is a z-score on test Y, and
N is the number of paired observations.

In Equation 7.2, the symbol *r* designates the correlation coefficient between two variables. Equation 7.2 also has a $z_x z_y$ term in the numerator. Such a term is referred to as a *cross-product.* A cross-product is the result of multiplication that takes place across the paired observations in two columns of numbers (such as the z-scores of –2.7 and –2.8 that the first person obtained on tests X and Y (see Table 7.1).

In this case, the two numbers being multiplied are z-scores. Σ, sigma, is an operator like + or –. It means to add up a set of numbers: In this instance, it means to add up the cross-products of the z-scores. Finally, *N* denotes the number of individuals in the sample: seven people drawn from a larger group.

Note that the correlation formula employs z-scores of the sort described in Chapters 5 and 6. That means that the original mean and standard deviations of the variables are entirely irrelevant to the correlation—in fact, they are not used when the two raw-score variables are translated to the universal language of z-scores. So, the correlation coefficient of two variables such as X and Y describes just the relationship between the two variables as they go up and down on a standard scale without reference to either original test's mean or standard deviation. This is why the relationship between the two variables is independent of the original scales of the tests. Put another way, the mean and standard deviation of the tests are irrelevant when it comes to relating two variables through a correlation coefficient.

Calculating the Correlation Coefficient From Z-Scores

We can see how Equation 7.2 is used by working through an example. Table 7.2 shows the data from five other people who took two tests X and Y. Using the methods described in Chapter 5, I have converted the raw scores on both tests to z-scores.

I have copied just the z-scores into Table 7.3 to make them easier to see.

In order to obtain the correlation, *r*, using the z-scores for the five individuals, we need three things. First, we need the cross-products of the zs. Second, we need to sum the cross-products. Third, we need to divide by the N.

The N (the number of paired observations, in this case) are the five paired observations, so N = 5.

Equation 7.2 is reprised in the text that follows for easy reference. As previously stated, the term on the upper left of the formula (Σ) indicates that we need to add up a series of numbers. Those numbers are a given participant's z-score on test X multiplied by the same participant's z-score on test Y—the cross-product.

Equation 7.2, reprised

$$r_{XY} = \frac{\sum z_x z_y}{N}$$

where:

r_{XY} is the correlation coefficient between scores on tests X and Y,
z_X is a z-score on test X,
z_Y is a z-score on test Y, and
N is the number of paired observations.

Table 7.4 shows the same data with the cross-products now filled in.

Table 7.2 From raw data to z-scores for variables X and Y, with observations of five people

	X Variable						Y Variable					
i	X	M	X–M	x^2	S	z_x	Y	M	Y–M	y^2	S	z_y
1	0	3	−3	9	2	−1.5	2	3	−1	1	2	−.5
2	2	3	−1	1	2	−.5	0	3	−3	9	2	−1.5
3	3	3	0	0	2	0	3	3	0	0	2	0
4	4	3	1	1	2	.5	6	3	3	1	2	1.5
5	6	3	3	9	2	1.5	4	3	1	9	2	.5
Σ	15	15	0	20	—	0	15	15	0	20	—	0
	$M = \Sigma X/N = 15/5 = 3$ $S^2 = \Sigma x^2/N = 20/5 = 4; S = 2$						$M = \Sigma Y/N = 15/5 = 3$ $S^2 = \Sigma y^2/N = 20/5 = 4; S = 2$					

Table 7.3 Scores for five participants who took tests X and Y, with their data converted to z-scores

i	z_x	z_y
1	−1.5	−.5
2	−.5	−1.5
3	0	0
4	.5	1.5
5	1.5	.5
Σ	0	0

Table 7.4 Scores for five participants who took tests X and Y, with their data converted to z-scores with cross-products

i	z_x	z_y	$z_x z_y$
1	−1.5	−.5	.75
2	−.5	−1.5	.75
3	0	0	.00
4	.5	1.5	.75
5	1.5	.5	.75
Σ	0	0	3.00
r = 3.00/5 = .60			

That is, each number in the right-most column is the product of the individual z_x and z_y scores multiplied together. For example, person 1's z-scores were −1.5 for Test X and −.5 on Test Y. The cross-product is .75 (−1.5 multiplied by −.5). That value appears in the $z_x z_y$ column.

Once that new column is complete, to get the correlation, all we need to do is add up the $z_x z_y$s (remember that the numerator of the equation was: $\Sigma z_x z_y$) and divide it by *N*. (Note: You should always multiply the individual cross-products first; then sum.) Doing so, we get 3.00/5 or .60, as our correlation coefficient.

A Graphical Approach to How the Correlation Coefficient Works

In this section, I will explore a second way of thinking about correlations —one that involves observing the scatterplot of the scores more closely. Let's return to the set of data in Table 7.1. These points had been graphed earlier in Figure 7.1. Beginning with an informal look at the z-score data in Table 7.1, it seems as if, when a score on X is low, so is the score on Y, and when X is high, Y is high as well. That suggests that the correlation coefficient will be positive (because the correlation is positive when two variables rise and fall together).

Figure 7.1 shows a scatterplot between the seven pairs of z-scores from Table 7.1 on tests X and Y. Each pair is designated by one position on the chart. For example, the first pair of z-scores was $z_x = -2.7$, $z_y = -2.8$. That pair is represented by the point shown at the far lower left position in the diagram. That point represents the intersection of a vertical line extending from −2.7 on the X axis and a horizontal line from −2.8 on the Y axis. Each point in the diagram similarly represents a pair of z-scores.

We can see how the index of relationship—the correlation coefficient—reflects this positive relationship by considering the graph in a bit more detail. Recall that the numerator of the correlation coefficient is dependent upon the sum of the cross-products of these pairs of scores. When $z_x z_y$ are both positive, they will appear in the upper right quadrant of a graph such as that shown in Figure 7.1. When multiplied together, they will result in positive numbers that contribute to a positive correlation.

When $z_x z_y$ are both negative, they will appear in the lower left quadrant of a graph such as that shown in Figure 7.1. When multiplied together, the two negative numbers *also* will result in positive numbers that contribute to the positive value of the correlation. (That is because two negative numbers multiplied together always equal a positive number.) So, points in the upper right and lower left quadrant, which represent the fact that the two variables go up and down together, will contribute to a higher positive correlation.

If, on the other hand, the points were clustered in the upper left and lower right quadrants of the graph (where there are no points), it would mean that when one z-score was positive, the other z-score was negative. Multiplying a positive and a negative z-score together would always result in a negative product. As a consequence, such a pattern would ensure a correlation with a *negative* value, meaning that as one test score went up, the other went down.

Finally, if the pairs of test scores are distributed all over the graph, the value of the correlation would trend toward zero, as positive and negative cross-products were added together and their signs cancelled one another out.

The scatterplot indicates why, when two variables go up and down together, they represent a positive relationship; when they move in the opposite direction, the correlation is negative; and when they are unrelated, the correlation is zero.

Correlations Among Test Items and Tests

Correlations Among Test Items Can Help Distinguish Good From Bad Items

Correlations among test items can tell us whether or not the items measure the same general concept. Each item on a spelling test ought to correlate with each other item on the test in a positive direction. Spelling "anoint" correctly should correlate with spelling "development" correctly and spelling "tyranny" correctly. Test developers typically correlate each test item with all the others.

Levels of correlations for individual test items are typically modest. The average correlation for items that measure mental abilities (i.e., criterion-report items) is often in the r = .05 to .25 range, occasionally trending upward to .35 or so. Item correlations are low for two reasons: First, areas of knowledge are vast and diverse. Knowing how to spell "anoint" does not necessary mean that one can spell "development" correctly. Second, individual items are subject to a great number of chance factors as a person responds to them. For that reason, ability tests are long, so as to collect responses to a large number of items. The large number of items allows the test-giver to collect a reasonable measure of a person's ability.

Other test items tend to have higher correlations. If a person is reporting on his or her mood state (i.e., process-report), and endorses an item such as *angry*, it is likely she also will endorse items such as *upset, frustrated*, and *aggravated*. For such items, correlations may be expected to be within a range of about .25 to .50 or higher. In this instance, we can think of the test as picking up a person's *theory of him- or herself*, which is, for many people, fairly consistent and broad.

Whatever the average level of the correlation among items—whether it is relatively low, as is generally the case with ability items, or somewhat higher, as is typical of self-judgments—each item is expected to correlate with its scale's total score. If an individual item is unrelated to the scale total, it likely is not contributing to good measurement and ought to be removed from the test. (I expand on this topic in Chapter 9.)

Correlations Can Identify Related Groups of Items

If a test measures more than one quality, it is usually divided into multiple scales. For example, a test of psychopathology might be composed of scales measuring schizophrenia and depression. In this case, depression scale items ought to correlate among themselves, and schizophrenia items ought to correlate among themselves, but the depression and schizophrenia items would be expected to correlate across scales at a lower level because the two concepts are mostly distinct. (There will be some overlap to the extent that individuals with schizophrenia may at times be depressed.) A mathematical technique known as *factor analysis* uses the correlations among items to help identify and confirm such patterns among correlations (see Chapter 9).

Correlations Can Relate Tests to One Another—and to Real-Life Criteria

Correlations are also employed to examine the degree to which one test correlates with another. For example, if test developers create two tests that they claim measure the same thing, the two tests ought to be fairly highly correlated. Two tests both claiming to measure extraversion, and defining it the same way, ought to correlate at $r = .60$ or above, and usually do. Intelligence tests such as the Stanford–Binet and the Wechsler intelligence scales often correlate in the high $r = .80$s or low .90s. Such high correlations among similar tests reassure us that tests claiming to measure the same qualities actually do so. The converse also is true: Tests measuring different variables should not correlate too highly with each other.

Most important, tests ought to predict real-life criteria. Intelligence tests should predict school grades, tests of extraversion should predict social behavior, and so on. The correlations between tests and real-life criteria are of considerable importance to demonstrating the utility of the testing enterprise.

A Few Cautions About Working With Correlations

There are times when correlation coefficients don't produce the results we would normally expect—and it's good to remember these issues as you work with them.

Correlations Work Best with Large Samples

First, correlations are most suited for calculations with large samples; they are notoriously variable when using samples of fewer than 100 people in size, and often vary substantially even in samples of 200 or 300. (The consistency of the estimate varies with the square root of N – 1). For that reason, psychometric techniques employing correlations should ideally begin with 100 participants or more, and may require observations upwards of 400, depending upon the research goal.

Selecting the best items for a test on the basis of correlations among items usually should not be considered until an *N* of 200 or 300 is reached; ideally 400. Sometimes, of course, researchers take the risk with lower *N*s, but they may be unpleasantly surprised later on.

The Problem of Outliers

A second issue with correlations is that they can be thrown off by extreme values. For that reason, it is often advisable to plot all the points and make sure that one extreme point isn't altering the pattern of the rest.

Restriction of Range

Third, the size of the correlations changes depending on the range of the two interrelated variables. *Restriction of range* refers to samples that lack relatively high- or low-scoring test-takers. Correlations are lower when there is a restriction of range in either or both of the tests' scores being measured. For example, if you are correlating IQ with grade-point average (GPA), the highest correlations are found among grade school children—who have a broad range of abilities. The correlation between IQ and GPA drops in college from high school because only the top two-thirds or one-half of all students go on to college—which results in a more restricted range of ability. McNemar (1969) offers a correction to the correlation coefficient due to such restriction of range.

The Strength of a Correlation Coefficient

If a test does predict a real-life criterion, what is the strength of the prediction and its practical application? For example, the SATs predict first-year college GPA at various colleges at about an $r = .40$ level. What does that level of correlation mean, exactly? There are at least four ways to view the level of a correlation coefficient.

Using the Level of the Correlation Itself

The most obvious way to describe the strength of a correlation is simply to report the correlation coefficient itself. Recall that the closer the correlation is to 1.0 (or −1.0), the stronger the relationship; conversely, the closer the correlation is to 0, the weaker the relationship. If the correlation is close to or exactly 1.0 or −1.0, the interpretation is fairly obvious: The relationship is perfect, or just about so. If the correlation is 0, the interpretation is also easy: there is no relationship. It is the in-between values that pose a greater issue of interpretation.

Intermediate values of the correlation coefficient neither correspond to anything (like percentages) that are easy to understand nor increase or decrease in equal intervals. Consider the $r = .40$ correlation between SAT scores and first-year college GPA. It is not possible to say that $r = .40$ means that 40 percent of the people are classified well. Nor can we say that a .80 correlation is twice as strong as a .40 correlation. So, other ways of communicating the intermediate values of correlations are used.

The Squared Correlation as an Index of Variance Explained

One approach to characterizing the strength of the relationship is to use the squared correlation as an index of the variance explained in the criterion. Statisticians agree that a correlation between two variables X and Y means that X can be said to explain a specific amount of the variance of the other variable, Y (and vice versa). The exact percentage of the variance explained in one variable by the other is given by taking the correlation coefficient, squaring it, and multiplying it by 100.

So, a correlation of .30 between variables X and Y means that variable X explains 9 percent of the variance (.30 squared times 100, or .09 × 100). That 9 percent is both the amount of variance that X explains of Y and that Y explains of X (explaining in either direction always is equivalent).

Given the SAT's $r = .40$ prediction of first-year-college GPA, the SAT accounts for 16 percent of the variance of that GPA (.40 squared is .16, and multiplied by 100 is 16 percent). This still leaves the question of what it means, exactly, to predict a percent of the variance.

Here is one way to think about it: First, each person's score varies from the mean to a certain degree. In variance terms, the average person varies from the mean in units that have been squared, summed, averaged, and then square-rooted, which results in the standard deviations.

If we think of an individual's deviation from the mean in terms of these squared, summed, averaged, and then square-rooted units, we can say that 16 percent of such a deviation is accounted for by the SAT. Imagine a college where the average first-year GPA was a 3.0, with a standard deviation of .6, and a variance of .36. If Jane obtained a first-year GPA of 3.72, then her deviation from the mean GPA is .72, or two times the variance. On average, we could estimate, 16 percent of that .72 upward shift, or about .115, can be explained by her SAT score.

Restated in general terms, the percentage of variance a test explains of a criterion can be made more concrete by thinking about individual cases as examples. In an individual's case, the percent of variance of the criterion explained can be thought of as the percent of the person's deviation from the mean on the criterion, as accounted for by the predictor variable. This accounting is only *on average* because the predictor variable may be more or less potent for a specific individual or subgroups of individuals.

If you find this a bit hard to follow, you are not alone ... which brings me to an alternative way to interpret the strength of a correlation coefficient: by graphing it.

Graphing the Correlation Coefficient

Another way to assess the strength of a correlation coefficient is to graph it and look at the points according to where they fall on the graph. If the points form a group in the shape of a line (or close to it), that is a strong relationship. To the degree the points vary from the line, the correlation is less strong. Upward sloping lines (from lower left to upper right) represent positive correlations; downward sloping lines (from upper left to lower right) represent negative correlations.

Graphing is a generally good approach to representing the strength of correlations. One drawback is that for the range of many real-life predictions—which is to say, between $r = .02$ and .40 (e.g., Mayer, 2001), such graphs often look more or less like a large jumble of points—and yet the relationships may nonetheless be very important. Graphing provides a good index (and is useful in explaining how a correlation coefficient works), but leaves open the question of how to discuss the practicality of the prediction, particularly at lower levels of correlations.

The Binomial Effect Size Display

The final approach I'll describe is referred to as a Binomial Effect Size Display (BESD, shown in Table 7.5). In the testing context, the BESD table divides people and their outcomes into those who scored high and low on the test (the rows), and those who were high and low on the outcome measure (the columns).

In Table 7.5, scores on a hypothetical *First Year Predictor Test* are divided (at the mean) into high- and low-scoring groups. The high test score row indicates the above average scorers on the First Year Test. The row beneath it indicates the below average scorers.

Table 7.5 A Binomial Effect Size Display Table for r = .00

		First-year college GPA		
		Low	High	Total
Scores on the First-Year Predictor Test	High	50	50	100
	Low	50	50	100
	Total	100	100	200

By convention, the BESD describes a sample of 200 people overall: 100 high scorers and 100 low scorers on the test. Because the sample is assumed to be perfectly normal, there always are equal numbers of participants above and below the test mean.

The columns of the BESD represent performance below or above a criterion, *first year college GPA* in this example. The participants are divided into those who were *low* and those who were *high* on the criterion.

Table 7.5 represents a baseline case: a BESD illustrating a zero correlation (r = 0) between the test and performance at the criterion. Because there is no relationship between the test and the criterion, participants are evenly distributed across the four cells. That is, people with high test scores were evenly divided between those who had high and low first-year college grades. Similarly, low test-scorers also were evenly divided. In this case, the test would not be useful as a tool to select people.

As the correlation rises from zero to a higher value, the cells in a BESD table change in a systematic way. If the correlation between the scores on the First-Year Predictor Test and first-year college grades was r = .10, the table would change slightly, with more high scorers showing high grades, and low scorers showing slightly lower grades (Table 7.6).

Table 7.6 A Binomial Effect Size Display Table for r = .10

		First-year college GPA		
		Low	**High**	**Total**
Scores on the First-Year Predictor Test	High	45	55	100
	Low	55	45	100
	Total	100	100	200

To adjust the table to reflect the correlation, these steps are employed:

1. Draw the standard BESD (already depicted in Table 7.5).
2. Find the correlation between the test and the criterion.
3. Divide the correlation in half.
4. Multiply it by 100.
5. Add and subtract the result from the middle four cells of the standard zero-correlation-based BESD, such that (assuming the correlation is

positive) there are more people who scored high on the test who succeeded and more people who scored low on the test who failed.

In the example just given, where $r = .10$, the .10 correlation is divided in half to yield .05. Next, .05 is multiplied by 100 to yield 5. In the final step we add 5 to the high and high and low and low cells, and subtract 5 from the high and low and low and high cells to yield the result.

This means that, of 100 high scorers on the First-Year Predictor Test, 55 will be judged as performing high on first-year grades, whereas only 45 of the low scorers on the test will be judged similarly.

Table 7.7 shows what happens for a correlation of $r = .40$ between scores on the First-Year Predictor Test and actual first-year GPAs at some colleges. The middle four cells are 30, 70, 70, and 30.

I obtained the numbers shown in Table 7.7 by taking the .40 correlation (for SATs), dividing it in half to get .20, multiplying it by 100 to get 20, and adding the resulting value (20) to the high and high and low and low cells (which started at 50) to get 70, and subtracting 20 from the high and low, and low and high cells (also starting at 50), to get 30. As mentioned earlier, this is near the actual level of prediction for the SAT.

A college that employed the SAT would be engaging in a far more successful selection process than one that used no predictive measures. If the college could admit only those students who scored high (i.e., above average) on the SAT, then 70 students of the incoming class would score above (the present) average, and only 30 below average, relative to a general sample (across all comparable colleges). This would allow more talented students to take advantage of the education the college provides, and protect other students from unnecessary failure.

Table 7.7 A Binomial Effect Size Display Table for r = .40

		First-year college GPA		
		Low	High	Total
Scores on the First-Year Predictor Test	High	30	70	100
	Low	70	30	100
	Total	100	100	200

The Binomial Effect Size Display table, relative to other approaches, allows for a more practical, pragmatic approach to explaining correlation by estimating what would happen in a selection process, if a test correlated with a criterion at a particular level.

Correlations Are Central to Psychometric Theory

Correlations of the sort described in this chapter play a central role in psychometric theory. For example, psychometric theory begins with an examination of the test score itself: how it can be divided into parts and what each part means. Understanding test scores, their parts, and the relationships among those parts involves thinking about the correlations among the parts. How it all works begins to unfold in the next chapter, in which psychometric theory is described in greater detail.

CHAPTER 8

What Does a Test Score Mean?

The Origin of Mental Measurement

The Beginnings of Psychometrics

Early in the 20th century, scientists were skeptical that any mental phenomena could be measured. The early advocates of mental tests gradually built a case that psychological measurement might plausibly work if carried out thoughtfully (Thurstone, 1928). To promote those aims, L. L. Thurstone (1932) laid out a remarkably clear treatment of how psychological measurement could take place: He organized the best of his course lectures on the topic in a textbook and presented virtually all the most important equations of classical psychometrics in use at his time (Thurstone, 1932).

Psychometrics is the name given to the study of psychological measurement, and particularly to the development and use of a family of mathematical models that describe tests and test scores, and how those test scores can be used to study people's psychological attributes. Psychologists who are experts in this area are known as psychometricians.

Psychometric Models: Classical Test Theory and Item Response Theory

Psychometrics today is made up of many branches of study, but we can distinguish two broad approaches. The first approach—the one that Thurstone wrote about—goes chiefly by the names of *Classical Test Theory* and *Classical True Score Theory* (CTT; the terms are used interchangeably). Classical Test Theory is most widely used and this chapter emphasizes the model. The second broad approach is *Item Response Theory* (or IRT). I will discuss IRT more fully in the next chapter and I will draw on concepts of IRT as I discuss test reliability and precision in Chapter 10. Classical Test Theory emerged first, and its widespread use makes it a good starting point for delving into how tests work.

The Foundations of Classical Test Theory

In the opening narrative of his 1932 work, Thurstone describes the predicament of the psychometrician who wants to assess a mental attribute. There were, according to Thurstone, just three things the measurer knew that were pertinent to his problem:

1. All measurement procedures are fallible. In all known instances of scientific measurement, errors are bound to occur.
2. The person possesses a real, actual level of the mental quality in question. That actual level of the attribute can be thought of as the individual's *true score* on the attribute. The true score can be measured by a psychological test, but only with some unknown degree of error.
3. The best antidote to the problem of error is to measure multiple times and then to average the results. By averaging together obtained imperfect measures, a closer approximation to the actual *true* value can be obtained, assuming some stability of the attribute over time.

These pieces of knowledge—that error exists, the idea of the true score, and the need to correct for error—suggests a possible measurement strategy that will be described further here.

Basic Assumptions and Definitions of Classical True Score Theory

The Five Assumptions

Thurstone's narrative covered several equations, which, when taken together, form the fundamental assumptions of Classical Test Theory (Allen & Yen, 1973, p. 57; Novick, 1965; Thurstone, 1932, p. 12). The knowledge that each measurement has some degree of error is formally reflected in what I refer to as the *fundamental equation of classical psychometrics*, Equation 8.1.

Equation 8.1, $X = T + E$, says that an obtained score on a test, X, is an additive combination of a person's true score, T—the *real* level of the variable—and some degree of error, E. In essence, the equation identifies the obtained value on the test and the true value, and labels the difference between them as error. Note that the error can be positive or negative, and therefore, the score obtained may be too high, too low, or just right.

Equation 8.1

$$X = T + E$$

where:
X is an obtained score on test X,
T is the true score on test X, and
E is an error score on test X.

Equation 8.1 captures the measurer's knowledge that any individual measurement is likely to diverge somewhat from the actual value.

From the perspective of a test-taker, the formula represents the possible difference between the answers she gave on the test, and the answers she might have given instead. For example, most people who take tests encounter questions for which deciding on the correct answer is difficult; they realize that even when making their best possible effort, they could have answered differently.

Consider the test item "Do you like parties? *Yes* or *No.*" For some individuals, this might trigger an inner monologue like this one:

> Well, how much do I have to like parties to answer *Yes*? I like some parties, but there are others I don't really like. And I like parties if I am feeling pretty good about myself at the time, am wearing some nice clothes, and am around some interesting people. But I don't like parties where people are flat-out drunk, or dull; those parties don't interest me at all. So, I'll say *Yes*, I like parties, but perhaps I should be saying *No* because there are a lot of parties I don't enjoy.

The fundamental equation X = T + E, tells us that the test-taker and test-maker share a common understanding, which I have offset for emphasis:

> Each obtained test score can be only partly accurate. Each score contains error that is due to chance considerations, including (in the case of self-judgments) personal deliberations of uncertain accuracy.

As a consequence, it helps to ask more than one question, worded in more than one way. (This explains why some tests have items that seem repetitive.)

The true score represents the test-taker's actual level of the mental quality under consideration. It can never be obtained directly. Remember, however, the measurer knows that a measurement can be improved by repeating it multiple times.

That idea—of multiple measurements—is captured in Equation 8.2: the second assumption of classical psychometrics.

Equation 8.2

$$\varepsilon(X) = T$$

where:
ε is the operator, meaning *expected value*,
X is an obtained score on test X, and
T is the true score on test X.

Equation 8.2 uses the symbol ε to indicate the *expected value*. The expected value can be thought of as the average of future scores a person might obtain on a series of similar tests (*Xs*).

Equation 8.2 states that if you administer the same kind of test to a person multiple times and then average the person's responses together, you will more and more closely approximate a person's true score. Pragmatically, if a person takes a dozen different adequate measures of the attribute, the true score is best estimated from the average of those test results.

The next three assumptions can be considered a kind of *mathematical housekeeping*. That is, although they are reasonable statements, their chief purpose is to permit the derivation of additional formulae that will collectively form the body of classical psychometrics.

The three assumptions are represented in Equations 8.3 to 8.5. Equation 8.3 tells us that the correlation between error scores and true scores on a test is zero (the two sets of scores are unrelated). Equation 8.4 tells us that the correlation between error scores on two different tests will be zero. Equation 8.5 tells us that the correlation is zero between error scores on one test and the true scores on a different test. Although these assumptions may not always be true, they are likely to be true, and they simplify the mathematics of classical test theory considerably. Like many other assumptions in statistics, minor violations often make little difference.

Equation 8.3

$$\rho_{ET} = 0$$

Equation 8.4

$$\rho_{E_1E_2} = 0$$

Equation 8.5

$$\rho_{E_1T_2} = 0$$

where:

ρ_{ET} is the population correlation between the error score and true score of an examinee on a test,

$\rho_{E_1E_2}$ is the population correlation between the error scores for an examinee on two different tests, and

$\rho_{E_1T_2}$ is the population correlation between an examinee's error score on one test and true score on a second test.

A Key Definition in Classical True Score Theory

Classical Test Theory also defines a special relationship between tests called *parallel tests.* Recall that there could exist multiple independent tests of the same attribute. That is, the theory allows for the possibility of multiple tests, each measuring the targeted true score to some degree.

Parallel tests are highly similar tests—so similar that psychometricians use a special set of symbols to represent them. Different tests are often symbolized X, Y, and Z. Tests that are parallel to test X are symbolized X′, X″, and so on. The true scores of parallel tests are denoted T, T′, and T″, and the error scores are denoted E, E′, and E″.

Keeping those symbols in mind, parallel tests are defined as follows:

> If two tests yield observed scores X and X′, and if the tests are consistent with the five assumptions above, and if, for the two tests, T = T′ and $\sigma^2_E = \sigma^2_{E'}$, then the tests are *parallel tests.*

That is, X and X′ refer to scores on two parallel tests. Their respective true scores, T and T′, are equal. Finally, σ^2_E and $\sigma^2_{E'}$ refer to the error variance of the two tests, and the definition states that those variances are equal as well.

But what do two parallel tests actually look like? To create parallel tests according to Classical Test Theory, psychometricians wrote tests in which each item on the parallel test X′ was paired with an item on the original test X. The paired items measured the same ability at approximately the same difficulty level, but the item on the parallel test X′ was a bit different from its pair-mate on the original test (X).

For example, two achievement tests, X and X′, might have items as shown in Table 8.1.

Consider the arithmetic item "Does 2 + 3 = 5?" A parallel test item might be "Does 3 + 2 = 5?" Or, consider the sociability item "Do you like parties? Yes or No." A parallel item might be "Do you like hanging out with large groups of friends? Yes or No."

So, starting with these three central ideas: X = T + E, $\varepsilon(X) = T$, and the idea of parallel tests, mathematicians derived interesting equations that collectively came to define classical psychometrics. One key element

Table 8.1 An example of parallel tests for second-grade math knowledge

Item	Test X	Parallel test X′
1.	What is 31 + 23?	What is 41 + 14?
2.	What is 23 − 15?	What is 21 − 14?
3.	What is 7 × 7?	What is 8 × 8?
4.	What is 8 + 7 + 6 + 5?	What is 3 + 4 + 5 + 6?
...	...	...

of this theory is the idea of *test reliability*. Test reliability provides an index of a test's precision of measurement.

Three Aspects of the Reliability Coefficient

Setting the Stage

Starting with the assumptions of Classical Test Score Theory, we can derive three formulae that together describe what reliability is and indicate how it can be measured. We start with an overview of what we are looking for. Table 8.2 shows a hypothetical instance of a sample of people who have taken three parallel tests yielding three scores. In addition, each person has a true score that represents his or her actual level on the attribute. There is only one true score—one true value, and we can't actually know it, but we can estimate it by taking the average of the obtained scores (see the rightmost column).

The psychometrician sets out to understand the correlation between a test and its true score. This is remarkable because the true score is a theoretical concept, which otherwise remains completely unknown. Each parallel test, X, X′, X″, and so on, will correlate with the true score at the same level. That is because any two parallel tests' true scores for a given person are the same by definition and the two tests also have the same error variance.

Estimating the Reliability From Correlations Between Parallel Tests

Thurstone worked through a series of derivations and arrived at the equations that helped to define what test reliability means—and to

Table 8.2 Hypothetical scores on parallel tests and true scores for a sample

The person	Scores on the parallel tests			The true scores
	X	X′	X″	T
Sam	12	11	13	12
Jane	14	15	13	14
Margaret	6	8	4	6
...	...	...	...	...

estimate it from parallel tests. First, Thurstone demonstrated that the correlation between any two parallel tests is equal to the squared correlation between the test and its own true score, as indicated in Equation 8.6. This result implies that unobservable scores—the true scores—have a defined, regular relationship with the test's observed scores; that relationship can be represented as a correlation coefficient. Since Thurstone's time, reliability has been defined as the square of the population correlation between a test's obtained and true scores. Put another way, reliability is a correlational index that reflects how closely related the obtained scores are to the true scores, and has a meaningful range from 0 to 1.0.

Equation 8.6

$$\rho_{XX'} = \rho^2_{XT}$$

where:

$\rho_{XX'}$ is the population correlation between scores on test, X, and scores on its parallel test, X′,

ρ^2_{XT} is the population correlation squared between scores on test X and the true scores on test X.

Thurstone also determined that reliability, $\rho_{XX'}$ represents the ratio of the true score variance to the obtained score variance. This relationship is shown in Equation 8.7. As the true score variance declines relative to the overall variance, reliability will drop. At zero, there will be no true score variance left—all the variance is due to error. At that point, the obtained scores on the test *cannot tell us about anything measured.* Because there is no such thing as a negative variance, the relationship cannot drop below zero (although, in practice, one does occasionally see such negative correlations, due to sampling variation).

Equation 8.7

$$\rho_{XX'} = \frac{\sigma^2_T}{\sigma^2_X}$$

where:

$\rho_{XX'}$ is the correlation between tests X and X′ (also, the reliability),
σ^2_T is the population variance of the true scores, and
σ^2_X is the population variance of the obtained scores.

Equations 8.6 and 8.7 also give us the very similar Equation 8.8.

Equation 8.8

$$\rho^2_{XT} = \frac{\sigma^2_T}{\sigma^2_X}$$

where:

$\rho^2_{XT'}$ is the population correlation squared between the obtained scores and true scores on test X (also, the reliability),
σ^2_T is the population variance of the true scores, and
σ^2_X is the population variance of the obtained scores.

Equation 8.8 tells us that the population correlation squared between the obtained test scores and its true scores also is equal to the variance of the true scores divided by the variance of the raw scores.

Three More Equations of General Use

Before leaving behind this treatment of classical psychometrics, two further equations are of general use. The first, Equation 8.9, is a very elegant one indeed. I present it here by itself, as its derivation takes us a bit far afield given what I have covered thus far. Equation 8.9 means that the variance of the obtained scores is equal to the sum of the variance of the true scores and the variance of the error scores. The equation is elegant in a variety of ways—for example, it mirrors X = T + E, so it is nice that it is also true (it didn't have to be).

Equation 8.9

$$\sigma_X^2 = \sigma_T^2 + \sigma_E^2$$

where:
σ_X^2 represents the variance of x,
σ_T^2 is the variance of the true scores, and
σ_E^2 represents the variance of error scores.

Equation 8.9 can be used to expand on the meaning of the ratio of σ^2_T/σ^2_X. For example, if you divide both sides of Equation 8.9 by σ^2_X and then subtract σ^2_E/σ^2_X from each side, you get Equation 8.10. This tells us that the ratio of the variance of the true scores to that of the obtained scores is equal to 1 minus the ratio of the variance of error scores to the variance of the obtained scores.

Equation 8.10

$$\rho_{XX'} = 1 - \frac{\sigma_E^2}{\sigma_X^2}$$

where:
σ_X^2 is the population variance of the obtained scores,
σ_E^2 is equal to the population variance of the error terms, and
$\rho_{XX'}$ is the population correlation between the obtained scores on parallel tests.

The further equation is 8.11. Building upon the equation above, this tells us that obtained scores are correlated to some degree with the test's error scores.

Equation 8.11

$$\rho^2_{XE} = \frac{\sigma^2_E}{\sigma^2_X}$$

where:

σ^2_X is the population variance of the obtained scores,

σ^2_E is equal to the population variance of the error terms, and

ρ^2_{XE} is the squared population correlation squared between the obtained and error scores.

Exploring the Relationship Between Test Length and Reliability

Some basics of the relationship between test length and reliability are shown in Equations 8.12 and 8.13 (after Equations 15 and 16 in Allen & Yen, 1979, p. 84). Read $\sigma^2_{E_X}$ as *the variance of the error scores on test X.* Read $\sigma^2_{T_X}$ as *the variance of the true scores on test X. K* represents the ratio of the test length of test X to Y. So, if test X is double the length of Y, then $K = 2$. If test X is triple the length of Y, then $K = 3$ and so on. You can then get a sense from Equations 8.12 and 8.13 of what happens as tests are lengthened.

As the length of test Y is multiplied *K* times, the variance of the test Y's error scores is multiplied by *K*. At first, that might appear discouraging—as a test is lengthened, the variance of the error score rises proportionally (Equation 8.12). But now look at Equation 8.13. As the length of the test rises to the same degree, the variance of the true score rises at the rate of K^2. In other words, as the test length grows, the obtained score is made up of increasingly more true score variance relative to error score.

This indicates that if a test is lengthened *K* times, two times ($K = 2$), or tripled in length ($K = 3$), then the relationship between the obtained score and error score also rises *K* times: two or three times. For the same lengthening, however, the relationship between the true score variance will rise *K*-squared times, that is by four times (i.e., 2^2) or by nine times (3^2). So, whenever we lengthen a test, the obtained score is made up of increasingly more true score variance relative to error score variance. That means that *as you lengthen a test that has any positive reliability, the reliability will rise*

Equation 8.12

$$\sigma^2_{E_X} = K\sigma^2_{E_Y}$$

Equation 8.13

$$\sigma^2_{T_X} = K^2\sigma^2_{T_Y}$$

where:

$\sigma^2_{E_X}$ is the variance of the error scores on test X,

$\sigma^2_{E_Y}$ is the variance of the error scores on test Y, a test $1/K$ in length relative to test X,

$\sigma^2_{T_X}$ is the variance of the true scores on text X,

$\sigma^2_{T_Y}$ is the variance of the true scores on test Y, a test $1/K$ in length relative to test X, and

K is the number of segments of test Y that equal the length of test X.

as well. This assumes, of course, that all the items function equally well. Item Response Theory adds in more considerations as to how to lengthen a test—covered next.

Lengthening of Tests: A Comparison of Classical Test Theory and Item Response Theory

As you can see in Classical Test Theory, the longer the test, the better it is. This simple relationship holds true in part because the classical model assumes that all the items are homogenous (the same). In Item Response Theory, however, items are dealt with in a more case-by-case manner and are no longer regarded as all equivalent. Rather, items vary in how well they distinguish test-takers of a given ability. For example, easier items help sort out test-takers of lower ability; harder items are more useful for sorting out test-takers of higher ability.

By carefully selecting the most informative items and ensuring that the items cover the full range of test-takers' ability levels, it is sometimes possible to overrule the "longer tests are more reliable" idea: Item Response

Theory analyses can create shorter tests that perform better than longer tests by carefully choosing individual items based on their performance.

Psychologists who use Classical Test Theory can do this to a degree as well by using techniques such as factor analysis discussed in Chapter 9, but Item Response Theory brings the practice of selecting items to a new level.

CHAPTER 9

Good Items and Latent Variables

Item Response Theory

The Origins of Item Response Theory

For much of the 20th century, psychometric analysis followed the rules of Classical Test Theory. Recently, however, our thinking about tests has been enriched by ideas from Item Response Theory (IRT). Although Item Response Theory can be depicted as an entirely new advance that arose from a group of independent thinkers (e.g., Embretson, 1996), I believe there is more continuity from Classical Test Theory to IRT than has been acknowledged. The developers of Item Response Theory were, after all, already experts in Classical Test Theory. Here, I will regard Item Response Theory as having evolved from Classical Test Theory—and as departing from the earlier theory by introducing a set of theoretical changes.

A Main Point of Classical Test Theory Revisited

To describe the transition from Classical Test Theory to Item Response Theory, recall that in Classical Test Theory, a person's obtained score on a test, X reflects her true score, T, plus an error score, E. In formulaic terms: $X = T + E$ (Equation 8.1). Item Response Theory reimagines this relationship in several important ways (while allowing the original relationship to remain true). I will present Item Response Theory as a series of steps from $X = T + E$ to new equations that help define a test-taker's answer to a test item.

First Theoretical Change: A Focus on Items

The first theoretical change introduced by IRT is to refocus our thinking from a test to the items that make it up. I have indicated the shift in Equation 9.1. The equation is the same as that in Equation 8.1, except that I have added the subscript "*item*" to reflect that we are now talking about a person's obtained score, X_{item} for an item, a corresponding true score T_{item} for the same item, and an error score E_{item} for the same item.

Psychometricians using Classical Test Theory had greater opportunity to examine the behavior of individual items on tests as the computing power available to them increased from the 1960s forward. They developed variations of their techniques increasingly focused on the item level, particularly certain forms of reliability calculations (coefficient alpha, examined in Chapter 10). This is one way in which Classical Test Theory built a foundation for Item Response Theory.

Equation 9.1

$$X_{item} = T_{item} + E_{item}$$

where:

X_{item} is an obtained score on an item from test X,
T_{item} is the true score on the same item from test X, and
E_{item} is an error score on the same item from test X.

Second Theoretical Change: Thinking About Item (and Test) Difficulty

A second, more profound change in thinking about tests was the inclusion of a new variable in the equation: test difficulty. As psychologists created parallel tests (to estimate test reliability), they noticed that difficulties often arose in doing so; in particular, one test was often harder than the other. Tests that were parallel in all respects except for being of different difficulties were called *essentially tau-equivalent* (see Graham, 2006, for more detail).

A test-taker's obtained score on a test, in other words, had to do not only with his true score but also with how hard the test was; that is, how likely a person was to "pass" the items (either to answer them correctly in the case of mental ability, or to agree with them in the case of self-judgment).

Consider the example depicted in Table 9.1 of Morgan and Taylor, who each took a scale measuring disagreeableness. Morgan took Test A and Taylor took Test B. The test items are along the left, and Morgan and Taylor's responses to them are recorded to the right. Both test-takers used the same response scale: They replied *0* for "Doesn't apply" and *1* for "Applies to me." Both Morgan and Taylor received the same score—a 3—on their respective tests. But are their levels of disagreeableness the same? Take a look at the tests in Table 9.1 and you decide.

If you are like most people, you decided that Taylor was more disagreeable than Morgan. You probably noticed that although the two test-takers answered the items identically, Taylor's items were *more difficult* as compared to Morgan's items—in the sense that people are less likely to agree with the items she agreed with. Taylor had to be more disagreeable

Table 9.1 Morgan and Taylor's scores for disagreeableness

Item stem	Item responses
Morgan's answers to Test A	
I sometimes point out when I think people are wrong.	1
Although I prefer to go along with the crowd, I will argue with other people if I feel a matter is important.	1
I distrust most people.	0
Even though I try to be flexible with friends, I know I can be firm if a matter is very important to me.	1
Morgan's score on test A	3
Taylor's answers to Test B	
I tell it like it is, regardless of people's feelings.	1
I am often uncompromising and argumentative.	1
I believe in never forgetting and never forgiving.	0
I stand my ground and I get my own way regardless of what others think.	1
Taylor's score on test B	3

Note: Response scale for both tests: 1 = Applies to me; 0 = Doesn't apply to me.

than Morgan to respond to her items in the way shown. Your reasoning employed what you knew about the item *difficulty* (in this case, the extremity of the statements).

To incorporate this idea into psychometric theory, we could imagine a modification of the fundamental equation $X = T + E$ in which we add a "B" term to reflect item difficulty, as in Equation 9.2.

Equation 9.2

$$X_{item} = T_{item} + E_{item} + B_{item}$$

where:

X_{item} is an obtained score on an item from test X,
T_{item} is the true score on the same item from test X,
E_{item} is an error score on the same item from test X and
B_{item} is the level of difficulty of the same item from test X.

Notes on the Terms "Item Difficulty," "Test-Taker Ability," and "Passing an Item" in Item Response Theory

Item Response Theory was initially developed with educational tests. In that context, high ability specifically referred to a test-taker's skill at answering questions correctly and item difficulty referred to how hard it was to answer a test item correctly. As psychologists applied Item Response Theory to more kinds of tests, they carried over the *ability* terminology to scales that measured other qualities such as extraversion and disagreeableness. In these contexts, ability became generalized to a person's level of a trait of any kind, and item difficulty was used to describe the likelihood of endorsing an item. In this new usage, an "easy" extraversion item might be "I sometimes like parties," because almost anyone likes some kinds of parties, and a "hard" extraversion item might be "I have enjoyed every party I have ever attended." The latter is identified as "hard" because most people are relatively unlikely to endorse or "pass" it—unless they are very high in extraversion indeed. With this understanding in mind, let's continue with the theoretical innovations of Item Response Theory.

Third Theoretical Change: The Choice of an Alternative Mathematical Model to the Linear Model

Item Response Theory also introduced a new mathematical model to replace the linear (additive) model of Classical Test Theory. To lay the groundwork for the change, I have rewritten Equation 9.2 ($X_{item} = T_{item} + E_{item} + B_{item}$) in a new version in Equation 9.3 that preserves the main terms (for now), but removes the addition signs. The equation states that the obtained score on an item is a function (f) of the person's true score, the error term E, and the item difficulty B. Note that the true score, which was denoted as T in Classical Test Theory, is denoted as θ (theta) in Item Response Theory.

Equation 9.3

$$X_{item} = f(\theta_{item}, E_{item}, B_{item})$$

where:

X_{item} is a person's obtained score on an item from test X,

f represents an (as-of-yet) unspecified function of the group of variables in the parentheses.

θ_{item} is the "theta" or true score on the same item from test X,

E_{item} is an error score on the same item from test X, and

B_{item} is the level of difficulty of the same item from test X.

Fourth Theoretical Change: Introducing the Probability of a "Correct" Response

Rather than speak of an obtained score, Item Response Theory speaks of the probability that a person with a given ability level (true score or theta, θ) will get the item correct. If there is only one item and the test-taker responds to the item just once, that obtained response is identical to the likelihood of getting the item correct. In that limited circumstance, the probability of getting the item correct, symbolized as $P|X_{correct}$, equals the test-taker's obtained score just as in Classical Test Theory. More generally, Item Response Theory estimates $P|X_{correct}$ (the probability of getting an item correct) from multiple scores.

Equation 9.4 shows this further alteration of the equation. Notice that I also have deleted the error term. In Item Response Theory, the error is included in the estimated probability, so there is no more need for an error term; error is built into the model in terms of probability.

Equation 9.4

$$(P|X_{item_{correct}}) = f(\theta_{item}, B_{item})$$

where:

$P|X_{item_{correct}}$ is the probability of getting an item correct (or endorsing it a certain way),

f represents an (as-of-yet) unspecified function of the group of variables in the parentheses.

θ_{item} is the "theta" or true score on the same item from test X, and

B_{item} is the level of difficulty of the same item from test X.

Whereas Classical Test Theory attributes fallibility to errors, in IRT error is a part of chance events, and sometimes by chance we attain a higher or lower score than is indicated by our ability. Item Response Theory attributes fallibility to the probabilistic nature of measurement and to the limitations of specific items that make up a test. Yes, this still sounds a lot like error.

Fifth Theoretical Change: Placing the Probability of Getting an Item Correct on a Logistic Scale

The Logit Scale

For every level of the person's ability, theta (θ), there is a given probability of a person answering a dichotomously scored item correctly that will range from 0 to 1, where 0 corresponds to no chance of success and 1 to a certainty of a correct answer. Consider the multiple-choice item "What is Item Response Theory?" followed by the four alternatives:

(a) a model (or set of related models) that concerns how test items and tests work

(b) a kind of educational program
(c) a theory of how people remember items
(d) none of the above

A test-taker will either be credited one point for the correct answer "a" (a model or models of how tests work), or zero points for any other less accurate answer.

Note that because this test item yields only two possible values (0 or 1) it is considered dichotomously scored. To keep matters simple, let's consider only dichotomously scored items in the following discussion, understanding that there are generalizations of this approach to other kinds of responses such as a Likert scale, where responses might range from 1 (strongly disagree) to 7 (strongly agree).

In certain Item Response Theory models, the probability of obtaining a correct score on an item, where probabilities vary from 0 to 1, is represented on a logistic or *logit scale.* When they are converted to a logistic scale, their values:

- vary from $-\infty$ to $+\infty$, but mostly from -3 to $+3$ (as with z-scores)
- are centered around zero
- form an equal interval scale measured in logits (*logit* is short for log-odds units) where 1 logit is similar to 1 standard deviation
- have a probability distribution similar to that of the normal curve (the logistic distribution tails are a bit narrower)

Three Steps From Probabilities to the Logit Function

We can transform our scores of 0 and 1 to the continuous logit function in three steps (O'Halloran, 2005, pp. 32–39).

In the first step, we assume a group of people have different ability levels in the area being measured. We further conclude that although the scores they earn on a given item are either 0 or 1, each person has an underlying probability of answering the item correctly. In the example in Table 9.2, I've chosen people with probabilities for getting an item correct beginning at 0 for a person with no ability in the area, and stepping up

Table 9.2 Converting probabilities to a logit function

	Step 1	Step 2	Step 3
Description of the step	Specify several probabilities to identify the curve.	Convert the probabilities to an odds ratio (p/(1−p)) to place them on a scale from 0 to ∞.	Take the natural log (ln) of the odds to create a symmetrical scale from −∞ to +∞.
Outcome	Probabilities	Odds ratio	Log odds units
Sample points along the curve	0	0:1→ 0	−∞
	.25	1:3→ 1/3	−1.1
	.5	1:1→ 1	0
	.75	3:1→ 3	1.1
	1.00	1:0→ +∞	∞

to 1 for a person who is always right, at .25 intervals for five points in all: 0, .25, .5, .75, and 1.00. (Different probabilities could have sufficed; my purpose at this point is to convert a few probabilities to allow me to sketch out the relationship between the probabilities and the log odds or logits.)

In the second step, the five probabilities are converted to corresponding odds ratios. For example, a probability of 0 means the odds of answering an item correctly are 0. A probability of .25, however, means the odds are 25:75, or 1:3 or .33. Converting from probabilities to odds has the effect of changing the probabilities from a scale of 0 to 1 to a scale that goes from 0 to +∞. (See the *Step 2* column of Table 9.2.)

In Step 3, we take the natural log of the odds ratio. This has the effect of changing the scale so that its new range is from −∞ to +∞. It also brings us to the logit scale.

The Formulae for the Cumulative Logit Curve

The formula for carrying out the steps shown in Table 9.2 is indicated in Equation 9.5—the equation for logit curve, otherwise known as the cumulative logit function. The left side of the equation refers specifically to the logits (log-odds-units on the X axis). For every logit, there is a different probability of correct responding, which is why the left side of Equation 9.1 reads *Logit(p)*—designating the logit that corresponds to a given probability. In this context, we are speaking of the probability of a correct answer on a test item.

Equation 9.5

$$Logit(p) = ln\left(\frac{p}{1-p}\right)$$

...where:

Logit (p) is the number on the logit scale that corresponds to a given proportion correct (in this context, the probability of getting an item correct),

ln is the natural logarithm of a number, and

p is the proportion correct.

The right side of the equation has two parts: *ln* instructs us to take the natural log of the terms in the parentheses. The parentheses, in turn, contain the conversion from the probability, *p*, to an odds ratio.

We can also graph the points from Table 9.2 (given by Equation 9.5) using the *probabilities* (or proportion correct) as the Y coordinates and the *log odds units* (or logits) as the X axis to see what cumulative logit function looks like; this is shown in Figure 9.1. It would be impractical to graph $-\infty$ or $+\infty$ (negative and positive infinity). Because the odds quickly become extremely low beyond −3 and extremely high beyond +3

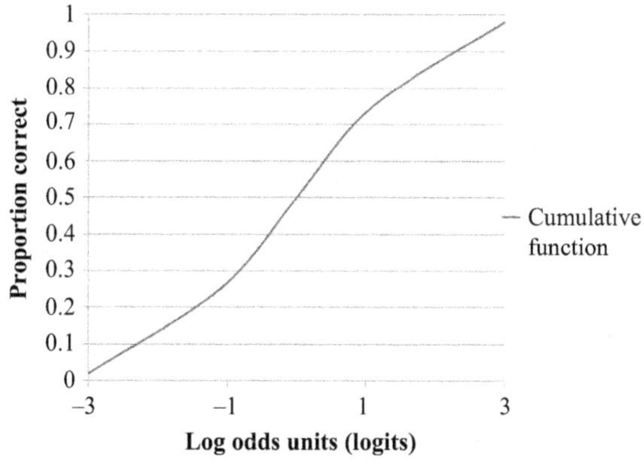

Figure 9.1 A cumulative logit curve

(as with z-scores), I have used points at ±3 as stand-ins for those infinite values.

Sixth Theoretical Change: Modeling the Likelihood of Answering an Item Correctly

With the foregoing changes, psychometricians are now in a position to estimate the likelihood that a test-taker will answer an item correctly. Item Response Theory uses a family of approaches called models to do this. The models commonly divide into one-, two-, and three-parameter models, named to reflect how many parameters (variables) are added to the basic logit function. I will focus on the one-parameter model in this introduction to IRT. The one-parameter model estimates the likelihood a person will answer an item correctly based on his ability level and the item's difficulty. (The two-parameter model adds in how well an item functions; the three-parameter model adds in a correction for guessing.)

Equation 9.6 shows this one-parameter model. The probability of getting an item right is a function of the test-taker's ability and of the item's difficulty.

Equation 9.6

$$P(\text{correct}|\theta) = \frac{1}{1+e^{-L}} = \frac{1}{1+e^{-1(\theta-\beta)}}$$

where:

P (correct|θ) is the likelihood a participant will answer the question correctly, given an ability level of θ,

L is the compound exponent (θ–β),

e is a numerical constant approximately equal to 2.718 called Euler's constant,

θ, theta is the latent variable representing a given level of test-taker's ability measured in logits, and

β, beta is the item difficulty measured in logits.

A One-Parameter Model of Test Items in Item Response Theory

Equation 9.6 shows the probability of getting an item correct given a person's ability level, P (correct|θ). That probability is a function of the person's ability level θ and the item difficulty β. These parameters appear together in the equation in the exponent in the formula's denominator as $\theta - \beta$. The exponent represents the difference between the test-taker's ability θ (theta), and the item's difficulty β (beta). The rest of the equation is taken up with the fixed values 1 and *e*; *e* stands for the numerical constant approximately equal to 2.718; this number is also known as Euler's number and is the base of the natural logarithm.

In Table 9.3, I have calculated the probability of answering two different items correctly for different levels of θ and β. People of seven different ability levels are depicted in the rows under the left-most

Table 9.3 The effect of item difficulty on the item characteristic curve

	Item 1 Difficulty Level, B = 0		**Item 2 Difficulty Level, B = 1**	
Ability Level (θ) in Logits	**Logistic deviate (solving for the exponent)**	**P(*Correct* | θ)**	**Logistic deviate (solving for the exponent)**	**P(*Correct* | θ)**
−3	−1(−3−0) = 3; e^3 = 20.1	1/(1 + 20.1) = .05	−1(−3−1) = 4; e^4 = 54.60	1/(1 + 54.6) = .02
−2	−1(−2−0) = 2; e^2 = 7.4	1/(1 + 7.4) = .12	−1(−2−1) = 3; e^3 = 20.1	1/(1 + 20.1) = .05
−1	−1(−1−0) = 1; e^1 = 2.7	1/(1 + 2.7) = .27	−1(1−1) =2; e^2 = 7.4	1/(1 + 7.4) = .12
0	−1(0−0) = 0; e^0 = 1	1/(1 + 1) = .5	−1(0−1) = 1; e^1 = 2.7	1/(1 + 2.7) = .27
1	−1(1−0) = −1; e^{-1} = 0.37	1/(1 + .37) = .73	−1(1−1) = 0; e^0 = 1	1/(1 + 1) = .5
2	−1(2−0) = −2; e^{-2} = 0.14	1/(1 + .14) = .88	−1(2−1) = −1; e^{-1} = 0.37	1/(1 + .37) = .73
3	−1(3−0) = −3; e^{-3} = 0.05	1/(1 + .05) = .95	−1(3−1) = −2; e^{-2} = 0.14	1/(1 + .14) = .88

column, where thetas (θs), or ability levels, take on the values of –3, –2, –1, 0, 1, 2, and 3, in the different rows (the treatment here follows Baker, 1985/2001, pp. 22–24.). Next, I have calculated the probability of answering the two items in the two columns labeled "Item 1" and "Item 2." Note that Item 1 is of average difficulty (β = 0); Item 2 is of greater difficulty (β = 1).

Under the "Item 1" heading are two subsidiary columns. The first subsidiary column shows the calculation of the value of the exponent, $-1(\theta - \beta)$; the second column has the complete answer—that is, the likelihood that a person with a given theta (as represented in the row) would get Item 1 correct. These computations are repeated for "Item 2" on the right-hand side.

Item Characteristic Curves

Figure 9.2 shows two *item characteristic curves* that correspond to Item 1 and Item 2, as depicted in Table 9.3. Item characteristic curves are used in Item Response Theory to represent the way individual items on a test behave. The item characteristic curve is a cumulative logit curve just like the one shown in Figure 9.1.

The item of average difficulty (β = 0) is at the center of the X axis. The harder item (β = 1) is shifted to the right. Although I didn't show an easier item here, if there were one it would be shifted to the left of center.

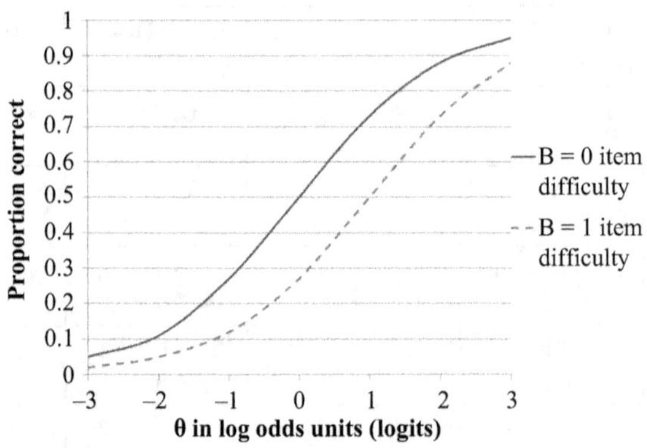

Figure 9.2 Item characteristic curves for two items of different difficulty levels

The item curves in Figure 9.2 tell us that people with higher θ (plotted on the X axis) are more likely to answer the items correctly (with the probability of a correct answer plotted on the Y axis). Participants with average levels of ability, shown when $\theta = 0$, are able to solve the average-difficulty item ($\beta = 0$) with a probability of .5, that is, 50 percent of the time, but they are able to solve the harder item ($\beta = 1$) with a somewhat lower probability of .27 or 27 percent of the time.

Seventh Theoretical Change: Using Item Characteristic Curves

Psychometricians examine item characteristic curves so as to select a good set of items that, collectively, will make a good test. By selecting items that represent a range of difficulties, they can measure the full spectrum of abilities, θ, that exist across people. As a consequence, tests developed with this model may better discriminate among test-takers and do so with fewer items than otherwise necessary. The spread of item difficulty also promotes more accurate measurement for participants at every level of ability—an advantage that is more difficult to ensure using Classical Test Theory alone.

Summing Up the Introduction to Item Response Theory

In the first part of this chapter, we have charted the transition from Classical Test Theory to Item Response Theory as a series of theoretical changes. The new Item Response Theory models allow test designers to take into account test-takers' abilities—as in Classical Test Theory—but also to consider item difficulties. This has the advantage of ensuring that a test measures well across the ability it targets. Two- and three-parameter models (not covered here) take into account item quality and test-takers' guessing. There are additional advantages to using IRT that are beyond the scope of this brief introduction (Embretson, 1996; Embretson & Herschberger, 1999). The chief drawback to Item Response Theory is its relative complexity. A central point here is that, despite their differences, there are many similarities between Classical Test Theory and Item Response Theory. One of those similarities is that both theories propose the existence of a latent variable—a hidden but very key attribute that represents a person's ability or level of a variable the test measures. The second half of this chapter turns to the nature of these latent variables.

Latent Variables

Describing Latent Variables

A *latent variable* is a hidden variable. Most important psychological variables are latent variables because we can never see directly inside the mind; rather, we form a conception of what we are searching for and then set out to assess it. To estimate a latent variable, we use indicators—most commonly test scores—to infer what is happening inside the mind.

As a concrete example, let's say we are trying to measure agreeableness. We might identify three different tests of agreeableness by three different test authors, where each test author uses a slightly different definition of the term. Next we might administer these three tests of agreeableness to a sample and obtain scores for each person on each test. The three measures we have taken are the *indicators* of agreeableness, and we can combine them by summing them (or by using more sophisticated techniques) to come up with an estimate of a person's *latent* degree of agreeableness.

We can reasonably claim that the true scores of Classical Test Theory are a special case of a latent variable—as are the thetas of Item Response Theory. In psychometric theories of all types, a true score (or theta) is estimated by a set of indicator variables—a group of items or tests that (we hope) are measuring a common attribute.

Latent Variables and Factor Analysis

The Number of Latent Variables That a Test Measures

Contemporary psychometric practice is to design a test scale so that it measures just one latent variable—but how can we be sure the test is assessing just one latent quality? For example, a test designer may be unsure how to measure extraversion. Perhaps extraversion is just one pure latent variable; in that case, the test-maker would create a single extraversion scale. However, extraversion could also be composed of two related latent variables: sociability and lively positive energy. In this latter case, the test-maker may be better off creating two subscales that measure the two attributes and can be combined as a measure of extraversion. To determine what makes the most sense, psychometricians examine the structure of the test.

Test Structure

Researchers examine a test's structure to understand how many *things*—latent variables—a test measures. The term test structure is short for *correlational* structure, which in turn refers to the pattern of correlations among the test items. (Alternatively, we speak of *covariance* structure; covariances are similar to correlations.)

To see how item correlations tell us about what a test measures, imagine for a moment that two items don't correlate. The items might be: "I am a reliable person" and "I am outgoing." We might conclude from their low correlation that one or both test items are bad (their error scores are high, in terms of classical psychometrics). A second possibility, however, is that both the items are good, but that they measure somewhat different latent variables—in this case, conscientiousness and extraversion.

Examining the remaining items on the test can help us decide which of these two alternatives is most likely. If the two items are simply bad, they won't correlate with anything else. But we may discover that the test is composed of two separate groups of items that correlate only moderately with one another. In such an instance, the test may be measuring two related latent variables rather than one.

The structure of a test refers to this pattern of how items are correlated with each other.

The Logic of Factor Analysis

By examining how the items correlate together, we can begin to understand how many things a test measures. The problem is that most tests are made up of large numbers of items, with even larger numbers of correlations—because every item is correlated with every other item. For that reason, psychologists use a technique called *factor analysis* to help them decide how many things a test measures. Factor analysis also can be used to understand how multiple tests relate to one another, but that is outside of our interests in this chapter.

The logic of factor analysis is straightforward: If test items are always answered the same way—that is, if they correlate relatively highly with one another—then they are said to measure the same thing. Conversely, if test-takers answer test items differently, they measure different things.

As an example, consider the very brief test of mood in Table 9.4. We might want to study mood to better understand the effect it has on performance—such as on the performance of athletic contenders. Before we get to that point, however, we want to know how many dimensions of mood our test really measures: Is there just one mood dimension, or are there many?

Consider the first two items, A and B, which inquire about happiness and contentedness. Most people are likely to answer these two items in the same way. A very cheerful person would probably agree with items A and B (responding with a *4* or *5*). A depressed person would probably disagree with both items A and B (responding with a *1* or *2*). According to the logic of factor analysis, because these items are likely answered the same way, they would be regarded as measuring the same thing. In the terminology of factor analysis, items A and B are said to measure one factor.

Now consider items C and D, which ask about energy and arousal. It is also likely that most people would answer these two items in about the same way. After all, an active or anxious person would feel both energetic and aroused (and mark *4* or *5*); a tired, sleepy person would feel neither (and mark *1* or *2*). According to the logic of factor analysis, we would therefore conclude that items C and D measure one single factor.

***Table 9.4* A mood test**

Item	Item stem	Item response
A	I am happy right now.	Disagree 1 2 3 4 5 Agree
B	I am content right now.	Disagree 1 2 3 4 5 Agree
C	I am energetic right now.	Disagree 1 2 3 4 5 Agree
D	I am aroused right now.	Disagree 1 2 3 4 5 Agree

Finally, compare items A and B with items C and D. People who agree or disagree with items A and B may or may not agree with items C and D. For example, a calm person may feel quite happy and content, but not feel aroused and energetic. Such a person would therefore agree with items A and B, but disagree with items C and D. On the other hand, a lively person may also feel happy and content, and also feel aroused and energetic. Such a person would agree with all four items. Or, an angry person might disagree with items A and B and also agree with items C and D, whereas a tired, depressed person might disagree with all four items. Because all of these possibilities exist, answers to items A and B tell us little or nothing about answers to items C and D. For that reason, items A and B are said to measure something different from items C and D, by the logic of factor analysis. Considering the four-item test as a whole from the perspective of factor analysis, we would say that its four items measure two factors: one by items A and B, and the second by items C and D.

Mathematically, the first step of a factor analysis involves taking a set of test items, administering them to a group of people, and then finding the correlations among the items. For example, the four-item test described above (i.e., *Happy*, *Content*, *Energetic*, and *Aroused*) might be given to 100 people, and then test data would be collected as in Table 9.5.

As we discussed earlier, people tend to give the same answer on items A and B, and the same answer on items C and D, but their answers to items A and B may be the same as or different from their answers to items C and D, because items A and B are unrelated to items C and D. The degree to which people give the same answers can be indexed with a

Table 9.5 Raw data matrix for a mood test

	Item A: Happy	**Item B: Content**	**Item C: Energetic**	**Item D: Aroused**
Person 1	5	5	1	1
Person 2	5	4	4	5
Person 3	1	2	3	3
Person 4	5	5	5	4
...	...	...	...	...
Person 100	1	1	1	1

correlation coefficient. The higher the correlation, the more people tend to give the same answers.

For example, in Table 9.5, people tended to answer questions A and B (and also, C and D) in the same ways. This shows up in the correlation matrix shown in Table 9.6. The columns are correlated with one another. Then the resulting correlations are arranged in a *correlation matrix*. A correlation matrix is simply a table designed to hold a set of correlations.

A correlation matrix is symmetrical, meaning that the upper right triangular portion of the matrix would mirror what you see in the lower left. For example, the correlation of *Happy* with *Content* is the same as the correlation between *Content* and *Happy*. For that reason, only one-half of the matrix is shown in Table 9.6. The cells of the table on the diagonal (from the upper left to the lower right) all contain 1.00, indicating that each variable correlates with itself perfectly.

The items *Happy* and *Content* correlate substantially (r = .40). The items *Energetic* and *Aroused* correlate highly as well (r = .39). But the *Happy* and *Content* items correlate lower with the *Energetic* (r = .10 and .10, respectively), or with the *Arousal* item (r = –.13 and –.01).

Why don't the items that we thought measure the same thing correlate more highly than r = .40, closer to r = 1.0? This occurs because each test item alone is very unreliable. You may recall from the earlier chapter on measurement that test reliability increases with test length. An individual item can be thought of as the shortest possible test that can be constructed—and hence the least reliable. Because individual items are so unreliable, their correlations with one another—even with very similar items—don't rise very high.

Even though the correlations between similar pairs (e.g., *Happy* and *Content*) are well below 1.0, they are still higher than the remainder of the correlations, which are close to 0 (between –.15 and +.15). It is

Table 9.6 Correlations among the mood test responses

	Happy	Content	Energetic	Aroused
Happy	1.00			
Content	.40	1.00		
Energetic	.10	.10	1.00	
Aroused	–.13	–.01	.39	1.00

this relative difference—comparing slightly higher to slightly lower correlations—that factor analysis uses.

The correlation matrix is another way of showing what we already suspected: Items A and B measure one thing, and items C and D measure a second, different thing. But note that we have now collected data that support the logical argument made above. Factor analysis can therefore provide empirical evidence of how many things a test measures.

What Factor Results Look Like and How to Interpret Them

If all the results were as clear as those in the correlation matrix, the analysis could stop here. But when a researcher is dealing with hundreds of items rather than only four, and when the correlations are closer together, the second step of factor analysis is useful.

The second step of a factor analysis is referred to as *extracting factors.* This is completed through the use of matrix algebra that is beyond the scope of this book. The result is a rearrangement of mathematical information, as shown in Table 9.7. Table 9.7 is referred to as a *factor-loading table.* It reveals: (a) the number of factors the test measures and (b) the correlation of the factors with the original variables.

This table reports that the mood test measures two factors. The first factor is highly correlated with the original items *Happy* and *Content*, and the second factor is highly correlated with the original items *Energetic* and *Aroused.* The correlation between a test item and a factor is called a *factor loading.* Based on these results, the researcher may wish to name the factors. For example, the researcher may refer to the first factor as *Pleasant Mood* and the second factor as *Aroused Mood.*

Table 9.7 Factor results for the brief mood scale

	Factor	
Item	**I**	**II**
Happy	.88	−.05
Content	.87	.23
Energetic	.15	.50
Aroused	−.08	.65

Correlations in the Original Correlation Matrix versus Correlations (Factor Loadings) in the Factor Table

As shown earlier, real-life data often includes some low correlations in the correlation matrix. These low correlations are due to the unreliability of the individual test items. No matter how high or low the correlations in the original correlation matrix may be, the factor loadings between items and the factors are almost always high (unless the factor is a weak one, or not really present). The reason that the correlations between items and factors are so much higher in the second step is that the factor analysis corrects for the unreliability of individual items. Typically correlations between items and factors above $r = .40$ are considered high; those below $r = .30$ are considered low.

Bipolar Factors and Negative Correlations

What about negative correlations among items? To explore this, let's return to the mood scale we first examined in Table 9.4 and add in a negatively correlating item, *Sad*, as indicated in Table 9.8, item E.

Table 9.8 An extended mood test

Item	Item stem	Item response
A	I am happy right now.	Disagree 1 2 3 4 5 Agree
B	I am content right now.	Disagree 1 2 3 4 5 Agree
C	I am energetic right now.	Disagree 1 2 3 4 5 Agree
D	I am aroused right now.	Disagree 1 2 3 4 5 Agree
E	I am sad right now.	Disagree 1 2 3 4 5 Agree

Now let's suppose that happy people (who agree with items A and B) will disagree with item E, *Sad*, and unhappy people will agree with item E, but disagree with items A and B. If our prediction is correct, then item E will correlate *negatively* with items A and B. This is because as E goes up, A and B will go down, and vice versa. If we test this empirically, we will obtain a correlation matrix such as the one in Table 9.9. The high negative correlations (i.e., $r = -.49, -.40$) indicate that there is a strong relationship between being happy and sad; they are just opposite sides of the same coin.

Table 9.9 Correlations among items from the extended mood test

	Happy	Content	Energetic	Aroused	Sad
Happy	1.00				
Content	.30	1.00			
Energetic	.05	.10	1.00		
Aroused	−.13	−.02	.39	1.00	
Sad	−.49	−.40	.07	−.03	1.00

Table 9.10 Factor results for the brief mood scale

	Factor	
Item	**I**	**II**
Happy	.88	−.05
Content	.87	.23
Energetic	.15	.50
Aroused	−.08	.65
Sad	−.85	.04

Repeating the second step of the factor analysis, the factor table would look like that shown in Table 9.10. Table 9.10 indicates that whenever *Happy* (and *Content*) feelings rise, endorsements for *Sad* decline, and vice versa. In the last section, the first factor was named *Pleasant Mood* and the second factor, *Aroused Mood.* With knowledge of the *Sad* item, the analyst might now want to rename the first factor *Pleasant-Unpleasant* (or *Happy-Sad*) *Mood,* to reflect the fact that it has definite meaning when it is high and low. This high-low quality is sometimes referred to as a *bipolar factor.*

Advanced Considerations With Factor Analysis

Factor analysis has many variations. For example, sometimes you may encounter discussions of factor *dimensions* and their *rotation.* These terms describe how factors can be interpreted as dimensions in space, according to advanced criteria drawn from geometry. When there are two factors, for example, they can be drawn in two dimensions. The practical value of these geometrical representations is that dimensions can then be rotated in space, changing factor loadings and thereby helping to clarify the theoretical interpretation of a factor. Another variation of factor analysis is to confirm the structure of a test, by predicting the test's factor structure ahead of time and then testing the prediction, an approach called *confirmatory factor analysis*. These considerations extend beyond the scope of this introduction to testing, but readers can consult further resources about factor analysis to learn more.

A Limit to the Logic of Factor Analysis

Factor analysis is a useful technique for clustering variables together according to the similarity they share with one another. But factor analysis may sometimes group together items, which, although highly correlated, are clearly theoretically distinct. For example, height and weight are highly correlated—the taller someone is, the more they weigh. And yet physicians would have overlooked very important aspects of personal health had they treated height and weight as equivalent—merely as an indication of size. Factor analysis may potentially combine together such variables, encouraging researchers to ignore the subtle (or not so subtle) distinctions between them. Prudence and theoretical savvy are useful when applying this technique.

Factor Analysis as a Foundation for Mental Tests

Almost every important mental test in use today is routinely subjected to factor analysis to check how many latent variables are being measured. A test can measure more than one latent variable, but if it does, the test can be strengthened with the creation of separate scales for each different variable. That is, researchers today often prefer to work with test scales that measure just one latent variable so as to be assured they are measuring one clearly defined quality of a person (Sijtsma & Junker, 2006).

Human mental life is complex and few scales are so pure that they measure one latent variable exclusively; rather, researchers aim for a scale to measure one factor predominantly—often using a rule of thumb of a greater than 3:1 ratio of the primary factor to any other factor that might be measured (Morizot, Ainsworth, & Reise, 2007). This ensures that the true score or the theta mostly represents what is being measured. Scales that meet or exceed this criterion are referred to as *unidimensional.*

From the Elements of Test Scores *to the* Elements of Test Quality

This chapter concludes our consideration of the elements of test scores. Psychometric theory divides the study of test scores into the latent variables they measure and their related qualities. Whatever branch of psychometrics we employ to study tests, the models we employ help us ensure that tests measure well. We turn to the elements of test quality in the final chapters of this book.

PART III

The Elements of Test Quality

CHAPTER 10

Reliability and Precision of Measurement

In Julius Caesar's time, Roman law specified that no army legion was permitted to cross the Rubicon River in the direction of the city of Rome itself. Crossing the 29-kilometer long river in northern Italy (perhaps the Pisciatello River on today's maps) would be an overt act of war. When General Julius Caesar crossed the Rubicon with his army, he intended to march toward Rome. He was reputed to have remarked, "The die is cast." Since that time, the expression "crossing the Rubicon" has meant a point of no return.

If you want to know the difference between a casual test and one that is suitable for scientific research, I would say that reporting the test's *reliability coefficient*—an index of how precisely the test measures—involves something analogous to crossing the Rubicon.

It is perfectly possible to write a test or quiz with little or no scientific understanding or no intention to conduct any research with it. These tests and quizzes show up as entertainment features in online quizzes and magazines ("What is your gardening IQ?"). Teachers have a weightier responsibility in developing fair and accurate tests for the classroom. Classroom instructors revise their exams based on their systematic observations of how students have performed on past tests.

When a researcher calculates a reliability coefficient for a measure and then reports it, however, she is making a more serious claim and crossing a Rubicon of sorts. Reporting such information implicitly indicates that the researcher (a) wants to go beyond the casual use of tests, (b) understands something about how tests work, (c) claims to know how to estimate reliability, and perhaps most important, (d) has administered the test to a sample of individuals and has succeeded in estimating its reliability.

When a test developer calculates the reliability of a test, she has an investment in it. Like Caesar and his army, there is no turning back: The test and its author must both be taken seriously and evaluated. Reliability is only a first step in establishing whether a test is worthwhile to use, but it is a tacit message from the test-maker: "I am serious about this test … … This test is worthy of scientific evaluation."

What Is Reliability?

A common-sense meaning of reliability is stability, dependability, and consistency. For example, if a 150-lb. person steps on a bathroom scale three times and obtains weights of 150, 151, and 150, the scale probably is reasonably reliable. If he steps on a different scale three times and obtains weights of 139, 161, and 151, the second scale would be considered less consistent and therefore less reliable.

These common-sense meanings are not far off from the technical meaning of test reliability: A reliable test will yield the same score for people with the same level of a given attribute each time it is given. These ideas are sometimes summarized as reflecting *consistency of measurement.*

Reliability Distinguished From Validity

If a test has a high level of reliability, it measures whatever it measures well. Note that reliability says absolutely nothing about *what* the test measures—the test could measure spelling ability or sobriety—it doesn't matter so far as reliability is concerned. *What* a test measures is a matter of its validity, and that is the topic of Chapter 11. Reliability concerns only the consistency with which the test measures.

Reliability also implies that an attribute is measured with *precision.* Precision refers to how close a test score is to the true value. Although reliability alone says nothing about *what* is measured, if a test exhibits reliability, it measures an attribute with a reasonable level of precision.

To understand more about reliability, this chapter will introduce several different forms of estimating the reliability of a test. Reading this chapter should provide you with a good sense of what reliability is—as well as the knowledge of how to calculate it.

Kinds of Test Reliability

There are many methods for estimating a test's reliability. Because this is an introduction to the topic, I'll limit the coverage in this chapter to a group of the most popular estimates here. These include: (a) parallel forms, (b) test-retest, (c) split-half approaches, and (d) coefficient alpha. Collectively, these cover most of the reliabilities reported in scientific research. Under many conditions, each of these methods yields roughly equivalent estimates of reliability. There are some qualities of each method, however, that are distinctive. Each method provides a unique perspective on the performance of a test.

Parallel Forms Reliability and the Classical Notion of the True Score (Revisited)

Description

Parallel forms reliability was the first method of estimating reliability developed in Classical Test Theory and is fundamental to the approach. From a historical perspective, it is the most basic type of reliability.

Recall that in Classical Test Theory the person to be studied is presumed to have a true level on a given variable under study (e.g., sensation-seeking), and this true level is designated as the true score, or T. The test-taker then takes a measure of sensation seeking. His obtained score, X, provides the measurer with an estimate of his true score, T. By repeating the measurement with a parallel test, X', a second estimate of T is obtained. If the two estimates for each person are similar across the sample of people, then the test has a good reliability.

If the measurer gives tests X and X′ to a number of people (say, 100), the measurer can calculate a correlation between the test scores X and X', which is denoted as $\rho_{XX'}$ or $r_{XX'}$. Remember that both $\rho_{XX'}$ and $r_{XX'}$ refer to the correlation between the two tests; ρ refers to the population value and r to the sample. Psychometricians tend to use symbols denoting the population when they are discussing reliability theory.

Psychometricians can prove mathematically that the correlation between two parallel tests is one good estimate of its reliability. The correlation between two parallel tests is also algebraically equivalent to the correlation squared between the test's raw scores, X, and true scores, T (see Equation 8.6). If the parallel tests correlate $r = .8$, for example, then test X estimates a person's true score, *T*, at the $r = .894$ level. If the tests correlate at lower levels, such as $r = .4$, they provide poorer estimates of *T*, at $r = .632$. The reliability for test X′, the parallel test, is the same as for test X. That is, if the two tests correlate $r = .8$, that is the reliability of both X and X′.

Parallel Forms Explained

The key to calculating a parallel tests estimate of reliability is (a) to obtain parallel forms of a test, and (b) to correlate them. A general procedure for creating parallel tests can be illustrated with the example of forming a vocabulary test and its parallel version. The test-maker first would write 100 *pairs* of items—as opposed to single items.

One member of an item pair might be "What is a mammal?"—which would be followed by one correct definition and three distracters. The paired vocabulary item might be "What is a reptile?"—which would also followed by a correct definition and three distracters. These two vocabulary items make a good pair because, for example, if you know the definition of a mammal, you typically understand how mammals differ from reptiles (and vice versa). That means the two questions are likely to be approximately equal in their difficulty level.

Next, the members of item pairs would be placed on test X or X′. To do this, a researcher might randomly permute the numbers 1 and 2 using a random-number generator, and obtain a list like {1 2}, {1 2}, {2 1}, and so on. Next, the researcher would assign *1* to test X and *2* to X′. Then, each pair of items would be assigned: If the mammal—reptile pair of questions were used, and the random numbers were {1 2}, then the mammal question would be assigned to test X and the reptile question to test X′.

Calculation

Once the test and its parallel test are created, the test-maker can then estimate the tests' reliabilities. First, the test and its parallel form are administered to the same large group of people. It's helpful to have a sample of at least 100, and preferably 400–500 people. Next, the researcher records each person's score on tests X and X′. The result is a set of paired observations for each person in the sample. Finally, the researcher correlates the participants' scores on test X with test X′. This correlation *is* the parallel forms estimate of the reliability.

Sometimes there are more than two parallel tests. In that case, there are several correlations among all the parallel tests. If there are more than two parallel tests, the estimate becomes the average of the correlations. (Some conversions may be necessary to average correlations; see a general introductory statistics book for these.)

We say that the correlation is *an estimate* of the reliability because it will deviate from complete accuracy due to sampling error and because reliability can be estimated in more than one way. Thus, the simple correlation between two parallel tests—or correlations among more parallel tests—provides an estimate of reliability, but other estimates are possible.

Parallel Forms and the Principle of Repeated Measurement

Each type of reliability examined in this chapter provides an insight into what reliability means and how reliability works. Recall that the fundamental equation of test theory is $X = T + E$ (Equation 8.1). The equation indicates that a person's obtained score is composed of a true score and an error score. The true score is constant across parallel measures, but the error score varies. So, if a test-taker took five parallel IQ tests, X, X′, X″, X‴, and X⁗, he might achieve scores of 115, 110, 120, 110, and 135, as shown in Table 10.1. Classical Test Theory (which we follow here) accepts such results by saying that the test-taker's true IQ (T) stayed the same, but the errors (E) varied across the parallel forms and their administrations.

Table 10.1 Administrations of five parallel tests to a single test-taker

	Administrations of parallel tests					
Type of score	X	X′	X″	X‴	X⁗	Average
Obtained (X)	115	110	120	110	135	118
True (T)	118	118	118	118	118	118
Error (E)	−3	−8	+2	−8	+17	0

Also according to Classical Test Theory, T = ε(X) (Equation 8.2); that is, the true score equals the expected value of X. The expected value, in turn, can be viewed as the average of obtained Xs on the IQ test.

In Table 10.1, the test-taker's five scores are averaged to obtain the best estimate of his true score. The average of the Xs is (115 + 110 + 120 + 110 + 135)/5 = 118.

In this example, each of the test-taker's scores on the parallel tests provides a reasonable estimate of his or her true score level, compared to some other alternatives we could imagine. For example, if the scores had been 100, 136, 0, 236, and 118 (which also average to 118), each individual estimate would be further off; that is, the errors would be larger. The estimates of reliability from the parallel tests would be lower as well.

As this example makes clear, reliability tells us the degree to which obtained scores on a test are relatively close to the true scores. The higher the reliability, the closer the obtained scores are to the true scores; the lower the reliability, the more random the relationship is between the obtained and true scores.

Evaluation

Classical Test Theory is founded on the idea of parallel tests. For many years, test-makers produced multiple, parallel versions of tests. For example, the widely used Stanford–Binet intelligence test was developed as two parallel forms, Forms L and M (Terman, 1942).

Parallel tests provide a way to assess a person's actual score on a test. The correlation between forms has a direct relationship with the correlation between the obtained and true scores. A test is said to be reliable if its true score and its obtained score have a very high correlation. So, a reliability of r = .90 indicates that a test is highly reliable, whereas a reliability of r = .00 indicates that it is not at all reliable. As measurement theory advanced, parallel forms became less important. For example, Forms L and M of the Stanford–Binet were later merged by combining the best parts of each test. This occurred as other methods for estimating reliability gained popularity.

Test-Retest Reliability

Description

The second approach to calculating reliability covered here yields a *test-retest* estimate of reliability. Test-retest reliability reflects the consistency of a test over time. In this approach to reliability, a single test is administered to a group of individuals, and then the same test (or a parallel version) is re-administered after some interval—typically a few days, weeks, or months. By re-administering the test at a later time, the test-taker's recall and practice effects are reduced or eliminated. If the same test is used twice (which is usually the case), it serves as a parallel version of itself.

If people never changed, this approach would be closely equivalent to parallel forms reliability. People do change, however, so this method offers some additional information that other estimates of reliability do not—a reliability that is estimated in the context of people's ongoing lives and reflects a person's potential changes.

For that reason, test-retest reliability tells us not only how reliable the test is in measuring an attribute, but also how consistent the feature being measured is over time. This approach, therefore, adds a very interesting and valuable source of information when evaluating a test's consistency of measurement.

Calculation

The test-retest reliability is calculated like the parallel forms reliability. It is a straightforward matter of correlating the paired scores on the test from time one to the scores on the same test (or a parallel version) collected at time two. The exact same test may be given twice, or, if parallel forms are available, one form might be given first and the other form second.

After the people's responses are gathered at each time, the researcher records each person's score on the test at times one and two; the correlation coefficient is then calculated for the paired observations. This correlation is itself the test-retest reliability estimate and requires no further adjustments.

Test-Retest Reliability and the Consistency of What Is Being Measured

A frequent premise of measurement and reliability estimates is that what is measured stays the same between measurements. For measures to be reliable over time, the target being measured must also remain mostly the same. Test-retest estimates of reliability can confirm such consistency—or indicate that an attribute is changeable.

For example, the test-retest reliability of a person's mood would be expected to be low on theoretical grounds, given that mood changes over time. As a second example, when conducting assessments of mental illness, a patient's presenting symptoms may change, sometimes dramatically. On one day, the patient may complain of lethargy and depression; a few days later, the patient may feel just fine. In such a case the test itself may not appear to be reliable, although its measurement properties may actually be acceptable. Such considerations must be factored into any consideration of test-retest reliability estimates and its alternatives.

Split-Half Reliability and the Prophets of Test Length: Approaching Internal Consistency

Description

Shortly after developing the parallel test approach, alternative methods were sought. After all, writing a parallel test can be a tedious and costly endeavor, as it requires writing many pairs of comparable items.

Some test developers asked, "Why not simply divide the already existing test in half, and use each half as a parallel test?" After all, they reasoned, the test is already created by one test author (or team) who compiled a group of items similar to one another to build the original test. So, if psychometricians divided the test into halves of equal length, wouldn't they obtain two parallel tests? It would be easy to divide the test into halves: you could divide the test into odd-numbered items and even-numbered items, or randomly assign half the items to each form.

The idea of dividing a test in half to make two parallel tests made a great deal of sense. And, if you correlate the two resulting halves, you surely would obtain an estimate of the reliability. However, the reliability estimate you obtained would be for a test *half the length* of the original, which raises the question: How does the reliability of a half test relate to the reliability of the original full-length version? More generally, how does test length relate to reliability?

Test Length and Reliability

Test reliability is closely related to test length. That is because each test *item* can be conceived of as an individual measure. In Classical Test Theory, the more items there are, the more measurements take place, and the higher the reliability will be.

The letter "K" is often used to designate a test's length: K might equal 10 items, in which case, $2K$ would represent a test length of 20 items, and $.5K$ would represent a test length of five items.

As the test length increases there are more items to sum. Both the true score variance and the error variance increase with the test's length—but the variance of the error scores rises directly as K increases, whereas the variance of the test's true scores rises faster at the rate of K squared (K^2). (These relationships are specified in Equations 8.12 and 8.13 in Chapter 8.) The test becomes more reliable as it is lengthened. We can use this principle to predict a test's full-length reliability from its halves.

Calculation of a Split-Half Reliability

To calculate the split-half reliability, a test first is administered to a sample of people. Then, the test is divided in half, for instance, into its odd and even items, and each person is assigned *two* scores—often, one based on the odd test items and one based on the even test items.

In the next step, a correlation is calculated for the relation between the scores on the odd and even halves. That correlation is the reliability of the *half test.* To estimate the reliability of the full-length test, we employ the Spearman–Brown Prophecy Formula. We can use a special case of the formula to estimate the reliability of any test that is split into two equal parts. The Spearman–Brown formula for this case is shown in Equation 10.1. The equation states that the reliability of the whole test is equal to the reliability of the half-length test multiplied by 2, and then divided by 1 plus the reliability of the half-length test.

For example, if the correlation between two test halves is .60, that is also the reliability of half the test. To estimate the reliability of the full-length test, we would multiply .60 by 2 and divide by 1 + .60, getting 1.20/1.60, or $r = .75$.

Equation 10.1

Spearman–Brown, Split-Half Form

$$\rho_{XX'} = \frac{2\rho_{HH'}}{1 + \rho_{HH'}}$$

where:

$\rho_{XX'}$ is the estimated reliability of a full-length test, and

$\rho_{HH'}$ is the correlation between test halves, and also the estimated reliability of the half test.

As a second example, if the reliability of the half test is .70, then the reliability of the original full-length test would be 1.40/1.70, or $r = .82$.

Table 10.2 shows how the reliability of a split half relates to the reliability of a full-length test. You can see that doubling a test's length always improves its reliability (assuming the new items are as good as the original ones). The improvement in reliability of doubling the test is

Table 10.2 The effect of doubling the length of a test on its reliability

Reliability of the original test	Estimated reliability for a test double the length
.10	.18
.20	.33
.30	.46
.40	.57
.50	.67
.60	.75
.70	.82
.80	.89
.90	.95

highest if the original test's reliability is around $r = .5$. If the original test's reliability is either much lower than .5 or much higher, then the effect of doubling its length is not quite so strong.

A more general form of the Spearman–Brown formula is shown in Equation 10.2. There, the *K* replaces the *2*, and other small modifications are made.

Equation 10.2

Spearman–Brown, General Form

$$\rho_{XX'} = \frac{K\rho_{part}}{1+(K-1)\rho_{part}}$$

where:

$\rho_{XX'}$ is the estimated reliability of a full length test,

ρ_{part} is the average correlation among the parts of the test, and

K is the number of parts.

Hint: Remember to add the *1* to the denominator *after* you have multiplied K – 1 times the average correlation.

The *K* in the formula now represents the number of times the test is lengthened. It might be 2 as in the earlier formula, 3, or 2.5. If the test is halved, *K* can be set to .5.

Using the general Spearman–Brown prophecy formula in Equation 10.2, consider a test developer who has a test of 30 items. The test developer wants to know what the reliability of the full 30-item-length test is and has administered his 30-item test to a sample of 150 individuals.

Next, he has divided up the test into three parts of 10 items and calculated each person's scores on the three parts. He found that the correlations among the three 10-item forms are .60, .55, and .65, yielding an average reliability of .60 across the three forms (it is sometimes preferable to transform the correlations for normality before averaging; see a standard statistics book for the *Fisher z transformation*).

To estimate the reliability of the total test, the researcher needs to know how much more reliable a 10-item test with a reliability of .60 would be when tripled (i.e., if *K* were equal to 3). In this instance, the numerator of Equation 10.2 would be 3 × .6 or 1.80, and the denominator would be 1 + 2(.6), or 2.20. The reliability of the triple-length test would therefore be 1.80/2.20, or .812.

K can also take on the value of a fraction (as already noted). Setting *K* to .5 can tell you what will happen to the reliability of a test if you divide the test in half. You might wish to do this with a test that is exceptionally long and requires several hours for a participant to complete. If the test has a reliability of $r = .96$, the new reliability would be found by multiplying the $r = .96$ by .5, yielding a numerator of .48. For the denominator, we would calculate 1 + ((.5 − 1) × .96), or 1 − .48, which yields .52. The final reliability estimate would be .48/.52, or .923. In other words, cutting the test in half would result in only a modest reduction in reliability.

Evaluation

The Spearman–Brown formula is very accurate, deviating from actual empirical findings sometimes by only a 100th or less. That is, if the formula predicts a full-scale reliability of .46, the actual value often will be somewhere between .45 and .47.

The split-half approach to estimating reliability made it possible to avoid the extra cost of developing parallel forms for each test. On the other hand, it introduced new issues. For example, although a test might be split into its odd and even items, it is often possible to split it in other ways as well. For example, a test-maker might take the first half of a test's items and correlate it with its second half, or employ other divisions. Each of the divisions will create a somewhat different split-half estimate of the reliability; often several split-half estimates of reliability are possible.

One way to avoid that problem is to use an alternative estimate of reliability called *coefficient alpha*.

Coefficient Alpha as an Index of Internal Consistency

Description

We learned in the previous section that the split-half approach can lead to more than one reliability estimate because there is more than one way to split a test. One solution to this problem is to take the average of all the possible split halves. An equation that yields a *lower bound* for this average is known as *coefficient alpha*. Coefficient alpha is a reliability estimate that takes into account the relationship among parts of the test. Those parts can be items, split quarters, split halves, or other splits. The description *lower bound* refers to the fact that Coefficient alpha is less than or equal to the lowest reliability estimate of a given test; it underestimates the test's reliability to the degree that the test items systematically differ from one another (Tavakol & Dennick, 2011). In such instances, the Spearman-Brown estimate may provide a superior estimate. Still, coefficient alpha is often the sole reliability estimate researchers report today.

A First Look at Coefficient Alpha—and the Relationship Between Variance and Reliability

As with the Spearman–Brown, coefficient alpha can be expressed in both a simplified form for a test with two parts, and a more general form that covers tests with more than two parts. The two-halves form is shown in Equation 10.3. The formula for coefficient alpha (Equation 10.3) looks

Equation 10.3
Coefficient Alpha, Split-Half Form

$$\rho_{XX'} \geq a = \frac{2[\sigma^2_{Tot} - (\sigma^2_{H_1} + \sigma^2_{H_2})]}{\sigma^2_{Tot}}$$

where:
$\rho_{XX'}$ is the reliability of the full-length test,
a is the estimated alpha coefficient reliability of the full-length test,
σ^2_{Tot} the variance of the total score,
$\sigma^2_{H_1}$ the variance of the first half of the test, and
$\sigma^2_{H_2}$ the variance of the second half of the test.
Note that in the equation, the greater than or equal to sign (≥) *refers to the fact that coefficient alpha estimates the lower bound of a reliability coefficient; the lower bound is less than or equal to other reliability estimates (see text).*

Table 10.3 A simple two-part test division to illustrate coefficient alpha

	Odd half of the test (H)	Even half of the test (H′)	Total test
	Items that make up the test portions		
	1, 3, and 5	2, 4, and 6	1, 2, 3, 4, 5, and 6
Test-taker (i)	*Test results for the test portions and test*		
1	1	3	4
2	2	4	6
3	2	5	7
4	0	1	1
...	...	...	...
100	2	4	6
Variances	1.5	3.5	6.5

quite different from any of the reliability coefficients encountered thus far. Coefficient alpha is, however, algebraically similar to other estimates of reliability and fits right into the family of reliabilities we are discussing.

Equation 10.3 states that coefficient alpha is equal to two times the variance of the whole test minus the sum of the variances of each test part, all divided by the variance of the whole test. This is quite different from the other ways of estimating reliability we have seen—this is the first time we have seen a reliability estimate without a correlation coefficient—so it makes sense to walk through an example of how the computation works.

A first common question about coefficient alpha concerns what the multiple variances in the formula refer to. To help answer the question, consider the situation depicted in Table 10.3. Table 10.3 portrays findings from a six-item test administered to 100 people (only results from the first four test-takers and the last test-taker are shown). The test has been split into odd and even halves, with items 1, 3, and 5 on the odd-numbered half and items 2, 4, and 6 on the even half. Test-taker 1 obtained a 1 on the odd half, a 3 on the even half, and a 4 on the total test. Test-taker 2 obtained a 2, 4, and 6, respectively. The total scores on these half-tests are shown in the middle columns. The variance of the odd half is 1.5, and of the even half is 3.5. In this instance, the sum of the first and second halves in Equation 10.3, $\sigma^2_{H_1}$ and $\sigma^2_{H_2}$, refer to the variance of the scores on the odd part of the test ($\sigma^2_{H_1}$ = 1.5) plus the variance of the scores on the even part of the test ($\sigma^2_{H_2}$ = 3.5). These sum to $\Sigma\sigma^2_{part}$ = 5.0. The right-most column of Table 10.3 contains scores on the total test, and $\Sigma\sigma_{Tot}$, refers to the variance of that column of total scores, which in this example is $\Sigma\sigma_{Tot}$ = 6.5. This total test variance, you might notice, is not simply the sum of the variances of the odd and even halves. Rather, the variance of the overall test score typically is greater in value than the sums of the variances of the odd and even halves. I will explain more about this next.

To understand why the total variance isn't (usually) just the sum of the variances of the parts, look at Equation 10.4, the general formula for adding two variances. Notice that the sum of the variances of the two parts of the test also includes a term reflecting the correlation between the two parts: The higher the correlation between the parts, the larger the term—and higher the total variance. Equation 10.4 tells us that as the correlation among parts increases, the variance of the total test increases as well. This makes sense, because if the two halves go up and down together, they will deviate further from their overall mean than if they were unrelated.

Equation 10.4

$$\sigma^2_{Tot} = \sigma^2_{H_1} + \sigma^2_{H_2} + 2\rho_{H_1 H_2}\sigma_{H_1}\sigma_{H_2}$$

Equation 10.5

$$\sigma^2_{Tot} = \sigma^2_{H_1} + \sigma^2_{H_2}$$

where:

σ^2_{Tot} is the variance of the total score,
$\sigma^2_{H_1}$ is the variance of the first half of the test,
$\sigma^2_{H_2}$ is the variance of the second half of the test,
σ_{H_1} is the standard deviation of the first half of the test,
σ_{H_2} is the standard deviation of the second half the test, and
$\rho_{H_1H_2}$ is the correlation between the two half-parts of the test.

Only in one limited instance, shown in Equation 10.5, will the sum of the variances equal the variance of the total test: when the correlation between the parts is zero and the third term drops out. In that instance, the test's overall reliability is zero.

This is how coefficient alpha *knows* the correlation between the items: It compares the ratio of the variance of the sum of individual parts of the test to the variance of the total test. As the total test variance rises higher than the sum of the variance of the parts, the correlation among the parts rises as well, yielding a positive estimate of reliability. If the total test variance really did equal only the sum of the parts (as in Equation 10.5), the test would have no reliability whatsoever.

Computing Coefficient Alpha

With this better understanding, let's refer again to Equation 10.3 (repeated here), and work through a problem. The equation states that coefficient alpha is equal to two times the total test variance minus the

Equation 10.3 (Reprised)

Coefficient Alpha, Split-Half Form

$$\rho_{XX'} \geq a = \frac{2[\sigma^2_{Tot} - (\sigma^2_{H_1} + \sigma^2_{H_2})]}{\sigma^2_{Tot}}$$

where:

$\rho_{XX'}$ is the reliability of the full-length test,

α is the estimated reliability of the full-length test,

σ^2_{Tot} the variance of the total score,

$\sigma^2_{H_1}$ the variance of the first half of the test, and

$\sigma^2_{H_2}$ the variance of the second half of the test.

**Note that in the equation, the* greater than or equal to sign (≥) *refers to the fact that coefficient alpha estimates the lower bound of a reliability coefficient; that is, the actual reliability is likely to be higher than alpha will estimate.*

sum of the variance of the two test halves, all divided by the total test variance (variance of the total scores). Table 10.3 gave an example of a two-part test with variances of 1.5 and 3.5 for the two parts, and a variance for the overall test of 6.5. Coefficient alpha would equal 2 [6.5 – 5]/6.5, or 3/6.5, or .54.

As a second example, if the variances of the two test parts were 15 and 20, and the variance for the total test was 60, alpha would be equal to 2[60 – (15 + 20)], divided by 60. Simplifying, one would obtain 2 × 25/60, or 50/60, or a total reliability of .83.

Consider the case where the sum of the variance of the parts equals the test's total variance. We know that such a relationship would hold only if the parts varied randomly in relation to one another (i.e., were uncorrelated). In such a case, the variance of the two part-tests might be 10 and 20, and that of the total test would be 30; alpha would equal 2[30 – (10 + 20)]/30, or (2 × 0)/30, which yields a reliability estimate of zero. Once again, it is this ratio that alpha "reads" to understand the correlation among parts.

Usually when coefficient alpha is applied, a more general form of the equation is employed, shown in Equation 10.6. Using this general form

Equation 10.6

Coefficient Alpha, General Form

$$\rho_{XX'} \geq a = \left[\frac{K}{K-1}\right]\left[\frac{\sigma^2_{Tot} - \Sigma\,\sigma^2_{Part}}{\sigma^2_{Tot}}\right]$$

where:

$\rho_{XX'}$ is the reliability of the full-length test,

α is the estimated reliability of the full-length test,

σ^2_{Tot} the variance of the total score,

σ^2_{Parts} the variance of the parts of the test, and

**Note that in the equation, the* greater than or equal to sign (≥) *refers to the fact that coefficient alpha estimates the lower bound of a reliability coefficient; that is, the actual reliability is likely to be higher than alpha will estimate.*

of alpha, a given test can be divided into its items (or some other division) and we can calculate the variance of each item of the test, and of the whole test. As before, *K* is the number of parts of the test. The variances of each part are added up in the numerator; the variance of the total test is the denominator.

For example, consider a four-item test where the four items have variances of 10, 9, 11, and 10, respectively, and the total test variance is 70. K in this case would be four, because there are four parts to the test. The sum of the variances of the parts of the test would equal 40 (that is, 10 + 9 + 11 + 10). Coefficient alpha, then, would equal 4/3 times (70 – 40)/70, or 1.33 × .429, or $\alpha = .57$.

Evaluation

Coefficient alpha is a useful tool when test items are homogeneous (measure the same thing). There are times, however, when an alpha estimate should not be used. This involves cases for which test items differ from one another in some systematic way: when, for example, they measure two related but distinct qualities. If an intelligence test is composed of both a vocabulary scale to measure verbal intelligence and a puzzle assembly task to measure mechanical intelligence, then a coefficient alpha reliability estimate will underestimate the reliability of the whole test because the two kinds of items will correlate less highly across tasks (i.e., from vocabulary to puzzles) than they do within the same area (e.g., vocabulary items with one another). In this case, reliabilities could be calculated separately for each subtest, but that still leaves the issue of how to estimate the reliability of the whole test.

One way to deal with a test with subareas is to employ the split-half reliability estimate and split the test in two so as to ensure that the two halves each contain half of the vocabulary and puzzle items—in essence, creating two parallel tests, and then applying the split-half correction. Another approach would be to use a test-retest method. Other methods involve more complex forms of reliability estimates, such as coefficient omega, which are beyond the scope of what is covered here in that they are computationally relatively complex (e.g., Sijtsma, 2009).

Measurement Precision

Precision and the Standard Error of Measurement

A test's *precision of measurement* refers to how precise its test scores are relative to the test-takers' true scores. The reliability of a test can be used in applied settings to estimate how precise a measurement is. In Classical Test Theory, each test has associated with it a *standard error of measurement,* which is defined as the standard deviation of the errors of the test scores. The equation for the standard error of measurement is shown in Equation 10.7.

Equation 10.7

$$SEM = S_E = S_X\sqrt{1 - r_{xx}}$$

where:

SEM and S_E both stand for the standard error of measurement,

S_X is the standard deviation of the test scores, and

r_{XX} is the estimated reliability of a full length test for a sample of participants.

Put into words, the standard error of measurement (SEM) equals the standard deviation of the test scores times the square root of 1 minus the reliability.

Test-makers can use the SEM to construct confidence intervals around a true score to see whether a person's obtained score might fall within a desired range. For example, a school for gifted children wishes to admit only students with a true score on an admissions test of 94 points or higher (out of 100); the SEM of the admissions test they employ is 6. If the school sets the minimum achievement level for entrance into the program at 90, what will be the likelihood of rejecting a child who is truly qualified—with a true score of 94 or higher?

The score of 90 is 4 points—or .67 SEM—below the target true score of 94. Twenty-five percent of the distribution of students with true scores of 94 is below that cutpoint of 90. We know this because, using a Z-test,

Z = (cutpoint – T)/SEM; that is, Z = (90 – 94)/6 = –4/6 = –67. The area under the unit normal curve between –∞ and –.67 is 25 percent. So, the probability that a person with a true achievement test score of 94 would be excluded from the program would be 25 percent. If the school administrators decide that the false exclusion rate is too high, they might lower the cutpoint to 88, 1 SEM below the target. That modification would reduce the false exclusion rate to 16%.

It is also possible to place a confidence interval around the participant's obtained score so as to estimate the range within which his true score fell (as opposed to this example, which placed a confidence interval around a true score). To do so requires a bit more calculation; details for how to do this can be found in Gullikson (1950) and Harvill (1991).

Item Response Theory and the Conditional Standard Error of Measurement

Item Response Theory provides a further refinement of precision in this regard. In Item Response Theory, items are ranked according to their level of difficulty and the precision of the test can be calculated at different score ranges. By convention, a test might be divided into 12 or 15 score ranges from the lowest to highest scores. Item Response Theory assesses the number of test items that provide information about performance at each difficulty level and the quality of those items. From such information, a *conditional* standard error of measurement can be calculated for each difficulty level of the test, and these are used to specify the precision of the test scores at each level. It turns out that, in practice, many tests measure more precisely at one range of scores than at another. For example, some achievement tests are very precise at measuring people with lower skill levels, but less precise at assessing those with higher levels of skills.

Meaning and Influence of Reliability

Test Reliability versus A Note on Inter-Judge (Scoring) Reliability

It is worth mentioning that the word *reliability* can be applied to other forms of consistency beyond those found *within* a test. For example, the term *reliability* is often applied to inter-judge agreement as to how to score a test. Inter-judge agreement refers not to the reliability of the test, but rather to the agreement between judges when scoring a test.

For example, in picture–story techniques such as the *Thematic Apperception Test,* a test-taker tells a story about an ambiguous picture such as a boy who is sitting at a piano. Then judges read the test-takers' stories and decide what motives might be represented; for example, how much the storyteller was thinking about the need to achieve. The degree to which the judges agree across stories can be considered an instance of inter-judge agreement or inter-judge reliability. Judges plainly must agree on their scoring for a test to work. To the extent that inter-judge reliability is low, it will detract from the reliability of the overall test because the stories cannot be adequately scored. But test items—the stories—must also exhibit test reliability. So reports of high inter-judge reliability (agreement) are insufficient in themselves to evaluate the reliability of a test, although they are certainly a necessary precondition.

Why Are Good Tests Reliable?

Why is reliability crucial? Remember that a test's true scores represent people's actual level of a psychological entity, be it need for achievement or extraversion. The reliability coefficient serves as an index of the correlation between the actual test scores and these hypothetical true scores. If the test's scores bear no relation to any true score, then the test is not measuring any attribute at all and should be discarded.

Test reliability is also key in that it limits the degree to which a test can predict (correlate with) an important outcome: A test cannot correlate with an outcome any more highly than the square root of its reliability. For example, if a test has a reliability of .5, it cannot correlate with an important criterion higher than .71 (the square root of .5). Fortunately, reliability provides a generous ceiling on such predictive relationships.

A further reason reliability is crucial is that it determines how accurate a test score is (on average) at an individual level. Reliability is a factor in estimating how close a person's obtained score on a test is to the individual's true score on the measured attribute.

For example, if an individual assessment is taking place, reliability should be high. For IQ or other personality assessments where some placement decisions might be made about an individual, a reliability of .85 or more may be considered necessary because reliability influences how accurately one can predict the individual's score.

Evaluating Reliabilities

Any person's obtained score is just an approximation of her true score. Tests that have very high reliability (typically above .80) often provide fairly good estimates of these underlying values. By comparison, if the test's reliability is between .65 and .79, its estimate of an individual's true ability is far more approximate. For that reason, it is important to use tests with good reliability when assessing individuals. Tests with lower reliabilities can still be useful in studying the relationships among variables in groups of people.

With these beginning principles, you should now be able to estimate reliability and also to use it to begin evaluating how good a test actually is. For example, many personality quizzes that appear in magazines have never had their reliability studied. For that reason, it is unclear if they measure *anything* of importance. In fact, a first question about how good a test is often comes down to: *What is its reliability?* A reliability estimate should be available to consider it a valid test. Reliability is, however, just one of the elements of a well-constructed test. It is a necessary criterion a test must meet, but insufficient by itself. There are additional, equally important criteria we need to understand before we consider a test worthwhile. These will be treated under the topic of validity, covered in Chapter 11.

CHAPTER 11

The Validity Movement

Issues of Validity

In the 19th century, professors graded college students on the basis of their in-class contributions, oral exams, short essays, and term papers. As classroom testing became more common in the early 20th century, students raised questions about whether the new multiple-choice tests and other newly introduced test formats worked. They requested accountability from their professors: Did multiple-choice tests really measure a student's knowledge? If so, how well could those tests assess their understanding?

Measurement specialists characterized the students' concerns as pertaining to the *validity* of a test. Test validity was defined in one early measurement textbook as "… whether a test really measures what it purports to measure" (Kelley, 1927, p. 14). Today, we often say the same thing: *A test is valid if it measures what it claims to measure.*

As educators and psychologists began to investigate test validity, an implicit social contract emerged between test-makers and test-takers: Students agreed to take the tests so long as experts agreed to maintain the quality of the tests they took—especially those measures' validity. The contract extended indefinitely into the future (Kelley, 1927, p. 14).

Individual tests have come and gone since those times and testing practices have changed. Through the years, the responsibility of test-makers to produce valid tests has remained a constant. To keep up with the changing nature of tests and testing environments, periodic revisions have been made to the standards by which the validity of mental tests are evaluated.

Test Validity and *Standards for Educational and Psychological Testing*

Test Standards

The key criteria that psychological tests must meet are found in a book entitled *Standards for Educational and Psychological Testing*. The standards were first published in 1966, and have been revised since then at roughly 15-year intervals. The most recent edition was developed by a joint committee of the American Psychological Association, the American Educational Research Association, and the National Council on Measurement in Education.

It may be impossible for any test to entirely satisfy all the desirable criteria outlined by the book's authors: The limits of scientific methods, scientific knowledge, and practical constraints including the cost of test development all place a limit on test quality. In that sense the *Standards* represent the aspirations of experts in testing as much as the realities of present-day tests. Regardless, good test publishers make information available about the degree to which their given tests meet the expert-developed criteria laid out in the work.

Changes in Test Standards Across the Years

Many luminaries in psychology have thought deeply about validity over the years. The philosophical nature of the question *What does it mean to measure something well?* allows for different opinions about how to approach the topic. The Joint Committee that has guided the *Standards* has changed its own views on key issues, sometimes dramatically, from edition to edition.

As a consequence, many academic articles about validity are consistent with some editions of the *Standards* but not with others. If you are a student of education or psychology, your professors likely taught you some version of validity standards. You will notice that longstanding beliefs about validity are sometimes revised in more recent versions of the *Standards*. For example, for 40 years or longer, professors taught topics such as *content validity* and *construct validity*. But the *Standards* of 1999 and 2014 argued those terms should no longer be employed: "There is only one validity," they stated, and therefore we should speak of "evidence for validity" from such sources as "test content" or the test's "correlations with criteria." Moreover, *construct validity*—which is discussed in countless articles—has been eliminated from the *Standards*, as it is now viewed as indistinguishable from overall validity.

A *Caution*

Even in a single edition, the *Standards* are not always consistent. The core definitions and arguments about validity can shift in slight but meaningful ways from passage to passage within the book. This is a consequence of the facts that experts don't always agree, that thinking about validity has changed over time, and that the Joint Committee that writes the *Standards* represents three organizations with different missions. In this chapter, I will try to capture the central views on validity in the current *Standards*, but please be advised that the work from which I summarize is open to different interpretations in places.

The Nature of Validity

Validity is at the heart of test measurement. We consider the question of validity as soon as a psychologist or educator claims that a test measures a particular attribute. For example, if a test-maker claims her test measures people's mathematical ability, then we must ask whether that claim is reasonable. According to the 2014 *Standards*:

> Validity refers to the degree to which evidence and theory support the interpretation of a test score for the proposed use of tests. (Joint Committee, 2014, p. 11)

Establishing validity requires a coherent argument that draws both on theoretical bases for the test as stated in the test manual or other sources, and the empirical findings from the research literature about the test. Validity is present only when theory and evidence jointly support the use of a test to measure what is claimed.

Constructs and Construct Representation

According to the *Standards,* tests measure *constructs.* The term *construct* is used synonymously with *concept.* In essence, a construct is a psychological attribute of a person: a hypothesized part of the mind that is measured (Joint Committee, 2014). Examples of constructs include arithmetic knowledge, extraversion, and social dominance (Cronbach & Meehl, 1955). A test is a valid measure when its scores substantially represent the targeted construct.

The current standards indicate that test scores can mismeasure in two ways: either (a) by not measuring enough of the construct under consideration, termed *construct underrepresentation,* or (b) by measuring too much of the wrong construct, which results in test scores containing *construct-irrelevant variance.*

Construct underrepresentation means that the test doesn't measure enough of the construct it tries to assess. For example, a test of sociability might measure just the desire to go to parties, omitting questions about whether someone likes to strike up conversations or to join groups of people for organized activities. A second example of this would be an intelligence test that measures only the ability to carry out mental arithmetic. In this case, the scale would overlook such important mental abilities as understanding vocabulary, carrying out visual reasoning, and other skills.

Construct-irrelevant variance refers to the degree to which test scores reflect something other than what the test is supposed to measure. If a test is supposed to measure an individual's actual mental ability, for example, but instead it asks the individual to *self-estimate* how smart she is, then the test will end up measuring the person's self-esteem more than her actual mental ability. Because self-esteem is irrelevant to actual mental ability—very smart people can be plagued with self-doubt—the test scores will reflect construct-irrelevant variance and be less valid on that account.

Validity is rarely an all-or-none proposition. A good test will represent the targeted construct to a reasonable degree, even though it may under-represent aspects of the attribute to be measured, or include some construct-irrelevant variance, or both. Validity exists along a continuum: The better the construct is measured by the test scores, the more valid the test (Joint Committee, 2014, p. 10).

Evidence for Validity

The validity of a test requires reasoning on the basis of evidence from a variety of sources. Chief among these are evidence from (a) test content, (b) response processes, (c) relationships with criteria, and (d) the internal structure of the measure.

Evidence from Test Content

Evidence for a test's validity rests, in part, on the test's content. Tests are more likely to be valid if their items directly address the topic being measured. For instance, the validity evidence for a test of agreeableness would be stronger if the test-makers directly asked questions about a person's agreeable thoughts and behavior than if the questions had to do with a test-taker's childhood. The evidence for validity would be more compelling still if the test-makers carefully defined the types of agreeableness they were trying to measure and then wrote items to cover each type of behavior.

Arnold Buss and Ann Durkee (1957) of the University of Texas carefully defined the content of their test of hostility. They first made a theoretical statement that hostility included: (a) assault on others, (b) indirect hostility (e.g., not helping a person who would otherwise be harmed), (c) irritability, (d) negativism, (e) resentment, (f) suspicion, and (g) verbal hostility. They then wrote a group of test items, being careful to include items that measured each of the respective areas. We can conclude that their test had well-chosen content that would count toward the measure's overall validity.

Evidence for validity from content is of special importance to educational tests. For example, if you want to know how much algebra an eighth-grader knows, it would be important to include algebra questions on an examination that reflect what is taught in the eighth grade.

Evidence Based on Response Processes

A second area of validity evidence concerns the kind of response process an examinee engages in when answering the questions on the test. A person's response process refers to the mental work the test-taker engages in to answer a test item. If a test-taker's processes are consistent with the test's measurement goals, our confidence in our interpretation of the test scores will increase.

If a test developer wants to explore whether his test measured the ability to carry numbers during addition (as opposed to having memorized answers to math problems), he could ask his second- and third-graders to talk aloud as they completed the problems. A student's talk-aloud response might be:

> Well let's see ... 9 + 4, that is going to be more than 10 so I am going to have to carry from the ones column to the tens column ... but how much? Well, I put a 3 in the ones column because 9 + 4 is three more than ten, and then a 1 in the tens column and 9 + 4 is 13.

The talk-aloud transcript provides good evidence that the test item elicited responses relevant to carrying numbers; several transcripts such as this one would provide good support for the test's validity.

Evidence for response validity (or its lack) can also be derived from well-established empirical findings. Dozens of studies make clear that people cannot reliably evaluate their own intelligence when asked how smart they are. Intelligence is more accurately measured by having people solve actual problems and determining how many of their answers are correct. Understanding these facts, if we encounter a test that asked, "How smart do you think you are?" we would realize it drew on self-evaluation—the wrong mental process for measuring intelligence—and we would argue that the test lacked validity. By comparison, asking people to solve problems and comparing their answers to the correct answers draws directly on the process needed to determine someone's intelligence (Mayer et al., 2008).

Evidence From Relationships With Criteria

A third area of evidence for a test's validity is reflected in how the test correlates with other variables. When we claim that a test measures a particular mental quality, our claim implies that the test ought to be correlated with other measures of that quality. For example, if we are examining the validity of a test of gratitude and we discover that people who score higher on the test expressed thanks to their friends on social media more frequently than low-scorers, that finding would support the test's validity.

I will divide the *Standards'* treatment of evidence from relations with criteria into three kinds of evidence: (a) correlations with other tests, (b) correlations with real-life criteria, and (c) differences in test scores across groups. Let's examine these in turn.

Correlations with Other Tests: Convergent and Discriminant Evidence

A test that exhibits correlations with other tests that measure the same construct has *convergent evidence* for its validity. Consider that corporations often give integrity tests to prospective employees; these tests are designed to measure whether a job applicant is honest, trustworthy, and reliable. If a test-maker developed a new integrity test, evidence for its validity would arise if it correlated with other existing measures of integrity and of conscientiousness (to which integrity is related).

Evidence for discriminant relations also can support the validity of a test. Discriminant evidence is important for demonstrating that a test is independent of tests that measure unrelated attributes. Continuing with the earlier example, an integrity test should exhibit low or near-zero correlations with measures of anxiety or hostility, attributes with which integrity is theoretically unrelated. Such a pattern would provide discriminant evidence for its validity.

As a second example, Larsen and Diener (1987) developed the *Affect Intensity Scale* to measure how intensely someone feels something. The test-makers wondered whether affect intensity overlapped too much with the concept of *neuroticism*. Neuroticism involves moodiness, high levels of negative emotions such as anxiety and anger, and similar qualities. As it turned out, the Affect Intensity Scale correlated only minimally with neuroticism, providing discriminant evidence that the Intensity Scale tapped a unique quality of personality.

Sometimes a seemingly valid test is later discovered to lack discriminant validity. The *Byrne Repression-Sensitization Scale* was designed to measure an individual's tendency to repress (block out) threatening thoughts. The scale items were carefully selected from a longer test—the Minnesota Multiphasic Personality Inventory. Byrne and his colleagues (Byrne, 1961; Byrne, Barry, & Nelson, 1963) conducted a number of studies all of which indicated that his scale measured repression. After work with the scale began, however, researchers learned that the Byrne scale correlated at levels around $r = .90$ with well-accepted measures of anxiety and neuroticism. Based on those findings, psychologists concluded that there was little unique in the scale beyond its measure of anxiety and it therefore lacked evidence for validity as a measure of repression (e.g., Slough, Kleinknecht, & Thorndike, 1984).

Correlations with Real-Life Criteria

In addition to exhibiting convergent and divergent correlations with other measures, a test should exhibit relations with real-life activities and outcomes. For example, a test of workplace integrity ought to correlate with an employee's on-the-job behavior: People who score higher on integrity should be involved in fewer instances of on-the-job theft. This turns out to be the case for such tests (Sackett & Schmidt, 2012).

As another example, intelligence tests are expected to correlate with grades in school. If they did not, evidence for their validity would be undermined. In fact, intelligence tests predict school grades at the $r = .50$ level. In addition, they correlate positively (very approximately) with larger brain size as determined by computerized tomography scans, as well as with people's speedier reaction times. The tests exhibit many similar patterns that collectively indicate that they actually measure what they are intended to measure.

Tests with good criterion evidence for their validity often are used for purposes of diagnosis and selection. Neuropsychological test scores contribute to decision-making as to whether a patient suffers from Alzheimer's disease; the aforementioned intelligence tests may help identify a gifted child who is wrongly placed in a class that is too easy for her.

Group Differences in Test Performance

The *Relations to Other Variables* category includes a final kind of evidence from group differences. Many tests claim to identify people who have certain personality characteristics, mental disorders, or the capacity for growth in a particular area. Evidence from group differences in test performance can support these claims. Consider a test for symptoms of paranoid personality disorder that measures suspiciousness and lack of trust. Empirical support for the test's validity can come from administering the test to a group of people who have been diagnosed with paranoid personality disorder and to a comparison group without the disorder. If the people diagnosed with paranoid personality disorder score higher on the test than the comparison group, the difference would provide evidence that the test is a measure of paranoid symptomatology.

Evidence From Internal Structure of the Measure

A further source of evidence for a test's validity concerns whether a test measures the same number of things it claims to measure. For example, if a test claims to measure three aspects of loving relationships—passion, intimacy, and commitment—does it really measure three fairly distinct and independent attributes? If the number of entities measured corresponds to the test-maker's claims, then the test has evidence for its structural validity. If there is a discrepancy between the claims about the number of features the test measures and its structure, then the test's validity could be lacking in this area.

Psychologists use factor analysis to determine the number of constructs a test measures. As discussed previously in Chapter 9, factor analysis is based on the idea that items measuring a given construct ought to correlate more highly with one another than do items that measure other constructs. A factor analysis of test items will group together the most similar (i.e., highly correlated) items by separating them from different ones. A pictorial representation of this relationship is shown in Figure 11.1 for a hypothetical test of intelligence that measures verbal, perceptual–organizational, and mental speed-related intelligences.

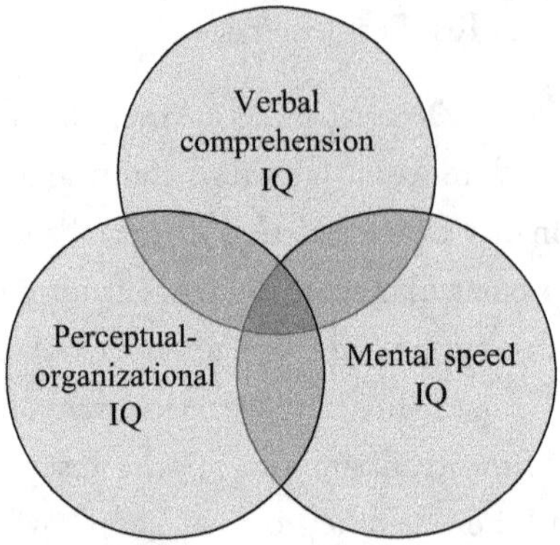

Figure 11.1 Partially independent subscales of a test provide evidence for the structural validity of the test

If the test's subscales correspond to the number of factors (i.e., constructs) that the test measures, then there is evidence the test's structure is as claimed. For example, if the test has three scales and the test items can be divided into three areas empirically, then the test is structurally valid. If there is considerable divergence between the number of constructs the test claims to measure and the actual number of factors, the test's validity would be questionable. For example, if a test has three scales but the test items appear to cluster into two or four areas, then validity evidence is reduced.

Integrating Findings Regarding the Test's Validity

The person evaluating a test's overall validity must sort through the evidence for each kind of validity, and then integrate the evidence into an overall conclusion regarding the validity of the test. Validity evidence is often complex and sometimes contradictory.

For example, a new test of extraversion may converge to a great extent with other similar tests. It also may predict important life outcomes related to extraversion. The test-makers may have claimed that they measure three areas of extraversion—high energy, talkativeness, and gregariousness—but show structural evidence for only two areas. In this case, the test evaluator must decide what evidence is most revealing of the scale's validity. Usually, a test's quality in terms of asking the right questions (evidence from content) and predicting important life outcomes (its correlation with social behavior) are of greatest importance. A lack of evidence concerning the test's specific structure deprives the specific subscales on the test of some validity, but does not necessarily limit the proper use of the overall scale.

Finally, when considering test validity, psychologists need to take into account the specific context in which a test will be employed. For example, tests that are valid under conditions of anonymity (e.g., surveys of drug use) may become invalid for job-selection purposes when anonymity is no longer a condition of testing. A college student might willingly acknowledge that he tried an illegal drug on an anonymous survey conducted at his university. He may later deny any drug use on an application for a job he strongly desires.

Given these complexities, it is not surprising that differences of opinion arise as to which tests are most appropriate for measuring an individual's attribute in a given situation. Still, there is usually a general consensus in an area as to which are the most and least valid tests for a specific purpose.

CHAPTER 12

The Elements of Better Testing

The Continuing Debate Over Tests

Echoes of Early Debates Over Testing

As testing became widespread in the 1920s, key debates arose between journalists and psychologists over its merits. In Chapter 1, I quoted Walter Lippmann's sentiment that "it would be a thousand times better if all the intelligence testers and all their questionnaires were sunk without warning in the Sargasso Sea" (Lippmann, 1922, p. 297). By the beginning of the 21st century, one could make a case that journalists, the public, and psychologists themselves understood tests and their proper use at least a little better.

The journalist Annie Paul recounted some of the history of psychological tests in her 2004 book, *The Cult of Personality*, and although she certainly criticized tests harshly at points, she also pointed out some of their merits. Her narrative describes the backgrounds of many tests and their developers that are relevant to our understanding of the instruments today. This is especially true in a broader context of understanding how tests work.

What is still left out of public discussion of tests today, as I see it, are good explanations of test validity and the broader standards of testing that good tests meet. There are but infrequent mentions of test validity in public commentary about testing, and often with little or no consideration of the meaning of the term. I have written this book in part to correct such omissions and to explain how tests work and the criteria they must meet.

Public criticisms of tests remain prevalent and—justified or not—they strike a particular chord of skepticism that the public has about tests and test results. Here I want to speak about several obstacles we all face in regard to accepting tests and what they tell us. I'll then address several ways to improve our testing practices (and how we communicate about tests), and conclude with a note about how tests can help us learn more about ourselves—and help us feel better as well.

Sources of Discomfort Over Tests

A substantial part of the public is still uncomfortable with the very notion of mental tests and there are multiple sources of our collective discomfort. Here are a few of the most important contributors.

Source 1: The Use of Tests for Selection

A key source of unease about tests—and one that is easy to understand—is that certain tests are used for high-stakes decision-making. Teachers use tests to identify the students in their class who have mastered the material and will get an A, the students who have done good work and will get a B, and the students who have done less well and will get lower grades.

College admissions officials use tests to choose the best and the brightest among their applicants and to turn away the rest. Psychiatrists and psychologists use mental tests to help them diagnose their patients with illnesses such as schizophrenia or borderline personality disorder. Employers use tests to select employees.

Professionals regularly employ our test scores to make consequential decisions about our lives. When their choices are contrary to our hopes, we can encounter unwanted obstacles along our chosen life path.

Source 2: The Personal Pain of Disappointing Feedback

When test results are used for selection and our scores are disappointing, they can cause us acute psychological pain along with surprise and even shock. Few of us want to hear we didn't get the job we applied for or that we are suffering from a mental disorder; similarly, very few of us want to hear anything negative about our personalities. People often blame the messenger: the test. It is human nature to reject certain forms of negative feedback. Bad news is often compounded by our emotional reactions to the rejection and our dashed expectations.

Above Average Expectations

A key finding by social psychologists is that most people in the Western world believe that they are above average on a wide variety of qualities. This is mathematically impossible. On average, people *are* average. When people anticipate that all their test scores will be above average and then receive actual results that don't match their expectations, they often experience more distress than they might have if their expectations were more realistic. Given such expectations, it is understandable to blame the test—illogical though that might be.

Problems with Test Feedback

Test administrators can sometimes compound people's apprehensive reactions by incompletely explaining a test result and failing to put it in context. Those who counsel people around test results need to ensure they do a good job of indicating (a) the fallibility of test scores, (b) what scores mean for a person, and (c) how a person can use such feedback to their benefit.

Many test results have positives that may become clearer with time, and test administrators can potentially help people see the value of the feedback. A young man might score highly on a scale of disagreeableness, for example, indicating that other people may perceive him as unfriendly, suspicious of others, and uncooperative. First of all, the young man is not necessarily going to be surprised by this: It may confirm something he has suspected of himself and in that sense be welcome. A professional providing feedback can ask about that, point out that disagreeableness has its virtuous side—for example, it helps people fend off unethical requests others make of them—and then explain that if a person wants to change his disagreeableness regardless of its advantages, he can become more agreeable over time if he chooses to do so.

Source 3: The Misuse of Tests

A further source of our unease about tests is that they are sometimes misused. Employers sometimes administer tests in a poor and thoughtless fashion, and use the tests in a highhanded and baseless manner to deny people jobs (Paul, 2004). Years ago, I visited a car dealership where the sales manager hired members of his sales force with the help of a "psychological test." He told me the test had been enormously successful in helping select his employees. When I asked him if I could see the test, he proudly produced a test with items designed to calculate a person's astrological sign. The sales manager was hiring only people born at certain times of the year. Apparently he was favoring Aries and Leos for their optimism, enthusiasm, and confidence (according to astrological thinking), and avoiding Pisces, who are allegedly more sensitive and unworldly. On the one hand, the sales manager's behavior was naïve and amusing; on the other, he had likely denied more than one perfectly qualified applicant a job. Moreover, the lack of connection between zodiac sign and sales performance made his use of the test indefensible.

Source 4: The Virtues of Egalitarianism

The national motto of France translates as *Liberty, equality, and brotherhood*—elevating equality to a national dream. The United States Declaration of Independence goes even further to declare that *all men are created equal*. It seems unlikely to me that the writers of France's motto and the U.S. Declaration of Independence really believed that everyone was the same—either at birth or beyond. Their purpose, rather, was to state emphatically that people ought to treat one another as though they are of equal worth. I agree with this sentiment, and yet I believe it is equally important that we recognize that we each have our own diverse mental and physical qualities. Part of treating one another as equal, to me, is acknowledging that each of us equally has our own specific needs, goals, and capabilities.

Yet some people, out of a disproportionate sense of equality (as I see it), argue that they are no different from anyone else—even in their mental abilities and other characteristics. I have met professors at Harvard and graduate students at Stanford who have told me something along the lines of, "I scored at a genius level of IQ, but it doesn't mean anything, of course." A member of a chatroom remarked online that he had an IQ of 149, and quickly added, "Regarding IQ tests, they certainly do not measure 'intelligence'; they are culturally biased and like someone said, they are pretty much just a predictor of how well someone will do in school, or on other IQ tests" (Synergy, 2007).

From the standpoint of the speaker, denying the importance of one's high IQ might seem like a decent tactic to reduce the possibility of intimidating others, but I find it problematic. *Of course* high scores on valid tests mean something. Luck, money, and social connections promote a person's success—and a person who lacks such resources will face much tougher odds to succeed. Without minimizing such social inequalities, we can also recognize that many individuals at prestigious universities earned their spots with more than luck and money alone: They also were smart. If we fail to acknowledge that reality, we are creating an inaccurate model of how the world works. Inaccurate understandings, in turn, create obstacles both to correctly interpreting test scores and more generally to how effectively we function in the world.

Such talented individuals might defend their choice (to deny their intelligence) by explaining that acknowledging their high abilities could create an awkward social distance between themselves and other people. For that same reason, students who attend prestigious universities such as Harvard or Yale often disguise their attainment by remarking that they go to college "in Boston" or "in New Haven" (Yoffe, 2014). That is their personal choice. I myself believe that greater openness and transparency in discussing individual differences can improve our understanding of one another.

Source 5: Resistance at the Level of Social Equity

Fairness to Groups

In the early part of the 20th century, certain intelligence tests (and perhaps other tests) possessed items that were biased against minority groups. Public commentators pointed this out and after several decades psychometricians responded by developing techniques to identify and then remove those unfair items from tests. The process begins with an examination of individual test items for content that might be unfair to any given group of test-takers, such as questions of general knowledge that might, for example, be better known by people of European than of Asian or African ancestry. After such a content analysis, test-makers routinely compare how test items are answered across groups and remove items that appear to unfairly disadvantage a particular group. Finally, test-makers ensure that tests predict consequential outcomes equally well for diverse groups. The procedures to identify and ameliorate test bias represented an important advance in the history, theory, and practice of testing.

People who remember that earlier era of testing may still hold beliefs—justified in earlier decades—that tests are biased in their measurement. Most experts in the area of test fairness agree that test bias against minority groups has been greatly reduced (some would say eliminated) in nationally used measures and most other measures. The persistent belief that such bias remains is yet another obstacle to the acceptance of tests. Today tests used for purposes of selection or other high-stakes evaluation are (in most instances) carefully developed with fairness in mind.

Source 6: A Sense of Too Many Tests and Too Much Testing

A newly emerging source of resistance to testing is the public perception that grade school students are taking too many tests at school. Parents believe—and some educators agree—that children are spending so much time taking tests that the teaching mission of these institutions is compromised as a consequence.

The increasing time spent on testing is of concern. Many students respond to tests with anxiety, and it is a rare student who finds tests fun to take. At the same time, evidence indicates that educational testing promotes learning. The mere act of taking a test can improve one's memory for the subject matter at hand because it provides practice at retrieving key information (Roediger & Karpicke, 2006). In the coming years, educators and testing services will do well to develop reasonable guidelines that balance learning and educational testing.

Source 7: A Lack of Test Literacy

Some professionals who think about tests on a regular basis—including journalists, lawyers, judges, and human resources professionals—are unsure of even the basic principles of how such tests operate. In high school biology, most of us are taught the principles underlying x-rays and CT scans. If we later encounter these medical tests as patients, we have some idea of how they function, which lets us face them with some calmness. Yet few of us are taught the psychometric principles underlying psychological tests. As a consequence, most of the public takes tests without knowing how they work. Public commentators often speak out about tests without reference to (or knowledge of) the well-worked-out standards of testing.

Fixing (Some) Problems

I believe mental tests represent an important scientific advance in the history of the human sciences, and that these measures have brought substantial gains both to individuals and to society. I am hopeful that by educating ourselves about tests, our public conversations about tests can evolve to a higher level. What follows is a short list of several changes that might help mitigate some of the above concerns.

Recommendation 1: Raise Test Literacy

Educators, journalists, and public commentators can help people understand more about the tests they take by helping to raise the public's literacy about psychological and educational tests. By increasing the test literacy of people in general, uninformed test critics will gradually be replaced by more knowledgeable ones and the quality of our conversations about tests will improve.

We will let go of debates over issues settled long ago, such as "Do tests work?" and "Is testing fair?" and move on to more productive issues such as "How can testing best help people?" "Which tests are best for a person at what times?" and "How can individuals and society as a whole best use tests?" I would like to extend my personal thanks to you as readers of this book for taking the time to consider how tests work.

Recommendation 2: Welcome Informed Skepticism About Tests

Test developers should welcome informed skepticism about their tests and be open to issues concerning the use of their test with specific individuals. Each of us has the responsibility to consider whether a given test score we receive is meaningful and useful to us. Good tests will work for the average test-taker, but none of us is exactly average. Each of us represents a specific personality within a particular context. A person with multiple sclerosis may, owing to the nature of her illness, have elevated scores on several scales of the Minnesota Multiphasic Personality Inventory (MMPI), which would suggest—erroneously—that she might also suffer from hypochondriasis, depression, hysteria, and schizophrenia (Hayes & Granello, 2009). Although the overall MMPI is valid, the test requires special consideration for patients with neurological disorders, and test interpreters must have enough sophistication to watch and account for exceptions like those.

There are also unknowns about how tests work for certain people. Most students I have taught over the years have earned scores on their SATs and GREs that were generally reflective of their abilities, as I saw it. Still, several students performed at a much brighter level academically than their scores would have predicted. In my experience, these test-takers are the exception rather than the rule among low scorers—yet, if my perceptions are correct, the existence of such test-takers reminds us our measures have room for improvement: Our present-day tests of mental ability simply don't seem to tap how this minority of test-takers think. I don't think anyone knows why.

To be clear, I am a firm believer in ability testing and the use of such tests. I do believe, however, in the value of regularly acknowledging that our understanding of people's mental qualities is incomplete.

In the meantime, we can also emphasize that mental life is multifaceted and that our assessments of an individual should include many features of personality. Keeping in mind the richness of our personalities can help us better appreciate an individual's overall psychological characteristics.

Recommendation 3: Teach Reasonable Expectations

I believe that we need to remind ourselves and teach our children that only about half the population will ever be above average (given normally distributed scores) at any one time. That means that roughly half the things we do in our lives will be above average and half below average. This is a sobering proposition, but we don't need to condemn ourselves or be shocked (or depressed or anxious) in its face. Rather, we may want to revive some old-fashioned coping mechanisms that healthy individuals have employed throughout time: focusing on competing against ourselves rather than against others, and on cultivating humility.

Recommendation 4: Improve Test Reports

In the early 20th century, psychiatrists and psychologists sometimes wrote assessments of their clients with a certitude that exaggerated what was known at the time and often failed to take into account the perspective of the test-taker. Isabel Briggs Myers, one of the co-authors of the Myers-Briggs Type Indicator, led the way towards a fairer, more engaging type of feedback (Paul, 2004). Myers wanted feedback that depicted "each [personality] type at its best, as exemplified by normal, well-balanced, well-adjusted, happy, and effective people." She crafted descriptions of a wide number of personality qualities that depicted the better (or, at least, neutral) side of human nature. Extroverts "like to focus on the outer world of people and activity," she wrote, while introverts "like to focus on their own inner world of ideas and experiences" (Paul, 2004, p. 112).

It is easier to write positive descriptions of extroverts and introverts than it is to write positive descriptions of people who fail classroom tests, who score at low levels on measures of intelligence, or who exhibit symptoms of serious psychopathology. In each of these contexts, however, test developers and those who administer tests can, should, and usually do work to communicate feedback in ways that are respectful of test-takers. Their respect toward the examinees may lead to the greater acceptance of tests over time.

Recommendation 5: Support the Collaborative Testing Movement

Those who administer tests can strive to collaborate as much as is possible with their clients. Even when testing is by its nature selective, as in the case of admissions officers choosing students for an incoming college class, or human resource officers selecting employees, there are techniques the assessor can use to lessen unpleasant results and their impact.

People who communicate test feedback can normalize the experience and point out potential positives from the process. Most of us experience a good deal of rejection in our lives and we survive it. As much as we might have our hearts set on one particular opportunity, tests may accurately reflect the possibility that other people may be more suitable for the opportunity to which we aspire. Someone else really may be a better match to our hoped-for school or to our hoped-for occupation. Even if we don't receive an offer of admission or of employment, the test may be telling us something useful: that we might need further preparation or, alternatively, that we might want to consider seeking a different course of study or career. Alternatively, of course, our test score (or the way it is used) might simply be wrong. Tests only tell us what is probable; that is the ambiguity of life. Either way, it may not hurt to at least consider whether we could meet our needs at an equal or higher level in some other way. A college applicant may find a similar school that is an equivalent or better match; the same may be true for a possible alternative career. Good test administrators can help people begin to think through the information they provide by forming a collaborative alliance with the test-taker. Adherents to the collaborative testing movement hope to explicitly develop this alliance between the testing expert and the client. I'll discuss this approach further shortly.

Recommendation 6: Ensure Test Fairness at the Social Level

Most tests today are carefully designed to ensure their fairness for different groups in our multicultural modern nations. That said, we should not relent in our efforts to ensure our tests are as fair as possible. Making tests as impartial as possible is a win-win proposition for both test developers and people who take tests. Continued vigilance in this area will work in everyone's favor.

The Collaborative Testing Movement

I am interested in people's abilities to understand their own and others' personalities—a capacity I refer to as *personal intelligence*—an intelligence about personality. I believe people who understand themselves and others have broad adaptive advantages in navigating their social worlds compared to those of us with less understanding (Mayer, 2014a; Mayer, 2014b).

I believe people can improve their self-understanding through the judicious use of psychological tests. That is one key reason I am a great supporter of the collaborative testing movement—the idea that coaches and mental health professionals can work together with their clients to help them learn from the testing process.

Finn and Tonsager (1992) developed a model of collaborative assessment called *therapeutic assessment*. In their approach, the test-taker and administrator first discuss the purpose of the assessment together. The client's questions about himself are taken seriously and tests are selected to focus on the client's questions. During the discussion, the assessor can introduce additional questions based on her expertise that could add to the client's self-knowledge through testing. Together, the client and assessor design a test battery that is guided by both of their interests and concerns. Such participative assessments have a number of advantages over the traditional expert-dictated approaches that were characteristic of psychological practice over much of the 20th century.

Poston and Hanson (2010) examined 17 clinical studies of the effects of psychological assessment as a therapeutic intervention. They found that therapeutic testing of the sort described above led to clinical improvements in therapy clients, and those effects were substantial. Using therapeutic testing led to a lessening of clients' symptoms: 86 percent of those undergoing therapeutic testing improved relative to the control group. A follow-up meta-analysis responding to criticisms of the first analyses yielded similar findings, suggesting that these findings are robust (Hanson & Poston, 2011; Lilienfeld, Garb, & Wood, 2011). Research on collaborative testing suggests that there may be a broader potential for people to benefit from the feedback that tests provide, so long as the assessment is performed well and the feedback is provided skillfully.

Concluding Comment

In this book, I have introduced the most important elements of psychological tests as I see them, including the elements of measurement, the elements of test scores, and the elements of good testing. The use of mental tests has generated an enormous amount of scholarly literature spanning dozens of journals and thousands of articles. In each area of this book, I have limited my focus to the most foundational ideas of test development and testing. By necessity, I have resisted delving into the many complexities of current theory, research, and practice in the area. For that reason, I have left more esoteric lines of test theory and tests untouched so as to focus solely on the essentials.

With those limitations acknowledged, this book represents one overview of the key building blocks of mental tests. Whether you complete your learning with this book or go on to learn more about the testing field, I hope this brief introduction will serve you well.

References

Accountemps. (2012, September 18). You had me at hello (news release). Retrieved from http://accountemps.rhi.mediaroom.com/interview-time

Ainsworth, M. D. S., Blehar, M. C., Waters, E., & Wall, S. (1978). *Patterns of attachment: A psychological study of the strange situation.* Hillsdale, NJ: Lawrence Erlbaum.

Allen, M. J., & Yen, W. M. (1979). *Introduction to measurement theory.* Monterey, CA: Brooks/Cole Publishing.

Anastasi, A., & Foley, J. P. (1949). *Differential psychology: Individual and group differences in behavior.* New York, NY: The MacMillan Company.

Aristotle. (1957/350 BCE). *On the soul, Parva naturalia, On breath.* Cambridge, MA: Harvard University Press.

Baker, F. B. (2001). *The basics of item response theory.* ERIC Clearinghouse one Assessment and Evaluation. Retrieved 1/2/2015 from http://info.worldbank.org/etools/docs/library/117765/Item%20Response%20Theory%20-%20F%20Baker.pdf (Original work published 1985, Heinemann)

Bartholomew, K., & Horowitz, L. M. (1991). Attachment styles among young adults: A test of a four-category model. *Journal of Personality & Social Psychology, 61*(2), 226–244. doi:10.1037/0022-3514.61.2.226

BBC News. (2000, August 10). Captain calamity strikes again. Retrieved 12/24/08 from: http://news.bbc.co.uk/2/hi/uk_news/872664.stm

Bowman, M. (1989). Testing individual differences in ancient China. *American Psychologist, 44*(3), 576–578. doi:10.1037/0003-066X.44.3.576.b

Buss, A. H., & Durkee, A. (1957). An inventory for assessing different kinds of hostility. *Journal of Consulting Psychology, 21,* 343–349.

Byrne, D. (1961). The repression-sensitization scale: Rationale, reliability and validity. *Journal of Personality, 29,* 334–339.

Byrne, D., Barry, J., & Nelson, D. (1963). Relation of the revised Repression-Sensitization Scale to measures of self-description. *Psychological Reports, 13,* 323–334.

Cable, D. M., & Judge, T. A. (1997). Interviewers' perceptions of person-organization fit and organizational selection decisions. *Journal of Applied Psychology, 79,* 998–1002. doi:10.1037/0021-9010.82.4.546

Carlson, R. E., Thayer, P. W., Mayfield, E. C., & Peterson, D. A. (1971). Improvements in the selection interview. *Personnel Journal, 50*(4), 268–275.

Carroll, J. B. (1995). Reflections on Stephen Jay Gould's *The Mismeasure of Man* (1981): A Retrospective Review. *Intelligence, 21,* 121–134.

Cheeseman Day, J., & Neuberger, E. C. (2002). *The big payoff: Educational attainment and synthetic estimates of work-life earnings.* U.S. Bureau of the Census, Special Reports (P23–210), Washington, DC: US Government Printing Office.

Conway, J. H., & Guy, R. K. (1996). *The book of numbers.* New York, NY: Springer-Verlag.

Conway, J. M., Jako, R. A., & Goodman, D. F. (1995). A meta-analysis of interrater and internal consistency reliability of selection interviews. *Journal of Applied Psychology, 80*(5), 565–579. doi:10.1037/0021-9010.80.5.565

Costa, P. T., & McCrae, R. R. (1992). *NEO PI-R professional manual.* Odessa, FL: Psychological Assessment Resources. Retrieved from http://www4.parinc.com

Cox, E. P. (1980). The optimal number of response alternatives for a scale: A review. *Journal of Marketing Research, 17*(4), 407–422. doi:10.2307/3150495

Cronbach, L. J., & Meehl, P. E. (1955). Construct validity in psychological tests. *Psychological Bulletin, 52*, 281–302.

Dahlstrom, W. G., Welsh, G. S., & Dahlstrom, L. E. (1972). *An MMPI handbook: Volume 1: Clinical interpretation.* Minneapolis, MN: University of Minnesota Press.

Der, G., & Deary, I. J. (2003). IQ, reaction time, and the differentiation hypothesis. *Intelligence, 31*(5), 491–503. doi:10.1016/S0160-2896(02)00189-7

Diodurus (1935/1960). *Diodurus of Sicily.* Cambridge, MA: Harvard University Press.

Dougherty, T. W., Turban, D. B., & Callender, J. C. (1994). Confirming first impressions in the employment interview: A field study of interviewer behavior. *Journal of Applied Psychology, 79*(5), 659–665. doi:10.1037/0021-9010.79.5.659

Ekman, P. (2001). *Telling lies: Clues to deceit in the marketplace, politics, and marriage.* New York, NY: W. W. Norton.

Ellenbogen, G. C. (1986). *Oral sadism and the vegetarian personality.* New York, NY: Brunner/Mazel.

Embretson, S. E. (1996). The new rules of measurement. *Psychological Assessment, 8*(4), 341–349. doi:10.1037/1040-3590.8.4.341

Embretson, S. E., & Hershberger, S. L. (Eds.) (1999). *The new rules of measurement: What every psychologist and educator should know.* New York, NY: Psychology Press.

Ericsson, K. A. (2002). Towards a procedure for eliciting verbal expression of non-verbal experience without reactivity: Interpreting the verbal overshadowing effect within the theortical framework for protocol analysis. *Applied Cognitive Psychology, 16*(8), 981–987. doi:10.1002/acp.925

Ericsson, K. A., & Simon, H. A. (1993). *Protocol analysis: Verbal reports as data* (Rev. ed.). Cambridge, MA: MIT Press.

•Eysenck, S. B. G., & Eysenck, H. J. (1963). The validity of questionnaire and rating assessments of extraversion and neuroticism, and their factorial stability. *British Journal of Psychology, 54*(1), 51–62. doi:10.1111/j.2044-8295.1963.tb00861.x

Fancher, R. E. (1987). The intelligence men: Makers of the IQ controversy. New York, NY: W. W. Norton. [Original work published 1985, Penguin].

Finn, S. E., & Tonsager, M. E. (1992). Therapeutic effects of providing MMPI-2 test feedback to college students awaiting therapy. *Psychological Assessment, 4*(3), 278–287. doi:10.1037/1040-3590.4.3.278

Foster, H. (1946). A comparative study of three tests for color vision. *Journal of Applied Psychology, 30*(2), 135–143. doi:10.1037/h0059525

Frank, L. K. (1939). Projective methods for the study of personality. *Journal of Psychology, 8*, 389–413. doi:http://dx.doi.org/10.1080/00223980.1939.9917671

Frazier, T. W. (2011). Introduction to the special section on advancing WAIS-IV and WMS-IV clinical interpretation. *Assessment, 18*, 131–132. doi:10.1177/1073191111408581

Funder, D. C. (1998). Why does personality psychology exist? *Psychological Inquiry, 9*(2), 150–152. doi:10.1207/s15327965pli0902_13

Gelade, G. (1995). Creative style and divergent production. *Journal of Creative Behavior, 29*(1), 36–53.

Gosling, S. D., Ko, S. J., & Mannarelli, T. (2002). A room with a cue: Personality judgments based on offices and bedrooms. *Journal of Personality & Social Psychology, 82*(3), 379–398. doi:10.1037/0022-3514.82.3.379

Graham, J. M. (2006). Congeneric and (essentially) tau-equivalent estimates of score reliability. What they are and how to use them. *Educational and Psychological Measurement, 66*, 930–944.

Griswold, C. L. (1986). *Self-knowledge in Plato's Phaedrus.* New Haven, CT: Yale University Press.

Guilford, J. P., & Fruchter, B. (1973). *Fundamental statistics in psychology and education.* (5th ed.). New York, NY: McGraw-Hill.

Gulliksen, H. (1950). *Theory of mental tests.* New York: John Wiley and Sons.

Hall, B. W. (1986). Validity, reliability, and norms of popular versus less popular published educational achievement tests. *Journal of Educational Research, 79*(3), 145–150.

Hanson, W. E., & Poston, J. M. (2011). Building confidence in psychological assessment as a therapeutic intervention: An empirically based reply to Lilienfeld, Garb, and Wood (2011). *Psychological Assessment, 23*(4), 1056–1062. doi:10.1037/a0025177

Harvill, L. M. (1991). NCME instructional module: Standard error of measurement. *Educational Measurement: Issues and Practice, 10,* 33–41.

Hayes, D., & Granello, D. H. (2009). Use of the Minnesota Multiphasic Personality Inventory-2 with persons diagnosed with multiple sclerosis. *Journal of Counseling & Development, 87*(2), 227–233. doi:10.1002/j.1556-6678.2009.tb00571.x

Higgins, C. A., Judge, T. A., & Ferris, G. R. (2003). Influence tactics and work outcomes: A meta-analysis. *Journal of Organizational Behavior, 24*(1), 89–106. doi:10.1002/job.181

Hiller, J. B., Rosenthal, R., & Bornstein, R. F. (1999). A comparative meta-analysis of Rorschach and MMPI. *Psychological Assessment, 11*(3), 278–296. doi:10.1037/1040-3590.11.3.278

Holland, J. L. (1997). *Making vocational choices: A theory of vocational personalities and work environments* (3rd ed.). Odessa, FL: Psychological Assessment Resources.

Holtzman, W. H. (2002). Over half a century of playing with inkblots and other wondrous pursuits. *Journal of Personality Assessment, 79*(1), 1–18. doi:10.1207/S15327752JPA7901_01

Jackson, D. N., & Messick, S. (1958). Content and style in personality assessment. *Psychological Bulletin, 55*(4), 243–252. doi:10.1037/h0045996

Joint Committee, (2014). *Standards for educational and psychological testing.* Washington, DC.

Judge, T. A., Higgins, C. A., & Cable, D. M. (2000). The employment interview: A review of recent research and recommendations for future research. *Human Resource Management Review, 10*(4), 383–406. doi:10.1016/S1053-4822(00)00033-4

Jung, C. G. (1973). Experimental researches including the studies in word association. In H. Read, M. Fordham & G. Adler (Eds.), *The collected works of C. G. Jung* (Vol. 2.) (pp. 3–317). Princeton, NJ: Princeton University Press.

Kelley, T. L. (1927). *Interpretation of educational measurements.* Yonkers-on-Hudson, NY: World Book Company.

Keyes, C. L. M., & Waterman, M. B. (2003). Dimensions of well-being and mental health in adulthood. In M. H. Bornstein, L Davidson, C. L. M. Keyes, & K. A. Moore (Eds.), *Well-being: Positive development across the life course* (pp. 477–497). Mahwah, NJ: Lawrence Erlbaum Associates.

Kleiman, L. S., & Faley, R. H. (1985). The implications of professional and legal guidelines for court decisions involving criterion-related validity: A review and analysis. *Personnel Psychology, 38*(4), 803–833. doi:10.1111/j.1744-6570.1985.tb00568.x

La Coste-Messelière, P. (1950). *The treasures of Delphi [Photographs by Georges de Miré*]. Paris: Éditions du Chêne.

Lacks, P. (1984). *A rational approach to the Bender.* New York, NY: John Wiley & Sons.

Larsen, R. J., & Diener, D. (1987). Affect intensity as an individual difference characteristic: A review. *Journal of Research in Personality, 21*(1), 1–39. doi:10.1016/0092-6566(87)90023-7

Lillienfeld, S. O., Garb, H. N., & Wood, J. M. (2011). Unresolved questions concerning the effectiveness of psychological assessment as a therapeutic intervention: Comment on Poston and Hanson (2010). *Psychological Assessment, 23*(4), 1047–1055. doi:10.1037/a0025177

Lippmann, W. (1922, November 22). The abuse of tests. *The New Republic, 32,* 297–298.

Lorge, I. (1951). The fundamental nature of measurement. In E. F. Lindquist (Ed.), *Educational measurement* (pp. 553–559). Washington, DC: American Council on Education.

Lubinski, D. (2000). Scientific and social significance of assessing individual differences: "Sinking shafts at a few critical points." *Annual Review of Psychology, 51,* 405–444. doi:10.1146/annurev.psych.51.1.405

Lubinski, D. (2004). Introduction to the special section on cognitive abilities: 100 years after Spearman's (1904) "'General intelligence,' objectively determined and measured." *Journal of Personality and Social Psychology, 86*(1), 96–111. doi:10.1037/0022-3514.86.1.96

Luskin, J. (1972). *Lippmann, liberty, and the press.* Tuscaloosa: The University of Alabama Press.

Mayer, J. D. (1995). A framework for the classification of personality components. *Journal of Personality, 63,* 819–877. doi:10.1111/j.1467-6494.1995.tb00318.x

Mayer, J. D. (2001). Primary divisions of personality and their scientific contributions: From the trilogy-of-mind to the systems set. *Journal for the Theory of Social Behaviour, 31*(4), 449–477. doi:10.1111/1468-5914.00169

Mayer, J. D. (2004). A classification system for the data of personality psychology and adjoining fields. *Review of General Psychology, 8*(3), 208–219. doi:10.1037/1089-2680.8.3.208

Mayer, J. D. (2005). A tale of two visions: Can a new view of personality help integrate psychology? *American Psychologist, 60*(4), 294–307. doi:10.1037/0003-066X.60.4.294

Mayer, J. D. (2014). *Personal intelligence: The power of personality and how it shapes our lives.* New York: Scientific American/Farrar, Straus & Giroux.

Mayer, J. D. (2015). The personality systems framework: Current theory and development. *Journal of Research in Personality, 56,* 4–14. doi:10.1016/j.jrp.2015.01.001

Mayer, J. D., Carlsmith, K. M., & Chabot, H. F. (1998). Describing the person's external environment: Conceptualizing and measuring the Life Space. *Journal of Research in Personality, 32*(3), 253–296. doi:10.1006/jrpe.1998.2220

Mayer, J. D., & Gaschke, Y. N. (1988). The experience and meta-experience of mood. *Journal of Personality and Social Psychology, 55*(1), 102–111. doi:10.1037/0022-3514.55.1.102

Mayer, J. D., Salovey, P., & Caruso, D. R. (2008). Emotional intelligence: New ability or eclectic traits? *American Psychologist, 63*(6), 503–517. doi:10.1037/0003-066X.63.6.503

McCann, J. T. (1998). Defending the Rorschach in court: An analysis using legal and professional standards. *Journal of Personality Assessment, 70*(1), 125–144. doi:10.1207/s15327752jpa7001_9

McClelland, D. C., & Koestner, R. (1992). The achievement motive. In C. P. Smith (Ed.), *Motivation and personality: Handbook of thematic content analysis* (pp. 143–152). New York, NY: Cambridge University Press. doi:10.1017/CBO9780511527937.010

Mayer, J. D., & Korogodsky, M. (2011). A really big picture of personality. *Social and Personality Psychology Compass, 5*(2), 104–117. doi:10.1111/j.1751-9004.2010.00336.x

McGrew, K. S. (2009). CHC theory and the human cognitive abilities project: Standing on the shoulders of the giants of psychometric intelligence research. *Intelligence, 37*(1), 1–10. doi:10.1016/j.intell.2008.08.004

McNemar, Q. (1969). *Psychological statistics* (4th ed.). New York, NY: John Wiley & Sons.

Meyer, G. J. (1997). Assessing reliability: Critical corrections for a critical examination of the Rorschach Comprehensive System. *Psychological Assessment, 9*(4), 480–489. doi:10.1037/1040-3590.9.4.480

Mischel, W., & Ebbesen, E. B. (1970). Attention in delay of gratification. *Journal of Personality and Social Psychology, 16*(2), 329–337. doi:10.1037/h0029815

Mischel, W., Shoda, Y., & Peake, P. K. (1988). The nature of adolescent competencies predicted by preschool delay of gratification. *Journal of Personality and Social Psychology, 54*(4), 687–696. doi:10.1037/0022-3514.54.4.687

Morizot, J., Ainsworth, A. T., & Reise, S. (2007). Toward modern psychometrics: Application of item response theory models in personality research. In R. W. Robins, R. C. Fraley, & R. F. Krueger (Eds.), *Handbook of research methods in personality psychology* (pp. 407–423). New York, NY: Guilford Press.

Murray, J. B. (1963). The MF Scale of the MMPI for college students. *Journal of Clinical Psychology, 19*(1), 113–115. doi:10.1002/1097-4679(196301)19:1<113::AID-JCLP2270190124>3.0.CO;2-D

Nisbett, R. E., Aronson, J., Blair, C., Dickens, W., Flynn, J., Halpern, D. F., & Turkheimer, E. (2012). Intelligence: New findings and theoretical developments. *American Psychologist, 67*(2), 130–159. doi:10.1037/a0026699

Nisbett, R. E., & Wilson, T. D. (1977). Telling more than we can know: Verbal reports on mental processes. *Psychological Review, 84*(3), 231–259. doi:10.1037/0033-295X.84.3.231

Norem, J. N. (2003). Pessimism: Accentuating the positive possibilities. In E. C. Chang & L. J. Sanna (Eds.), *Virtue, vice, and personality: The complexity of behavior* (pp. 91–104). Washington, DC: American Psychological Association. doi:10.1037/10614-006

Novick, M. R. (1965). The axioms and principal results of classical test theory. *ETS Research Bulletin Series, 1*. Published online 2014, 8 August. Retrieved from http://onlinelibrary.wiley.com/doi/10.1002/j.2333-8504.1965.tb00132.x/pdf

Nowlis, V. (1965). Research with the mood adjective check list. In S. Tomkins & C. Izard (Eds.), *Affect, cognition, and personality.* New York, NY: Springer.

Nunnally, J. C. (1978). *Psychometric theory* (2nd ed.). New York, NY: McGraw Hill.

O'Halloran, S. (2005). Lecture 9: Logit/Probit. [Sustainable Development U9611 Econometrics II]. PDF online. Retrieved from http://www.columbia.edu/~so33/SusDev/Lecture_9.pdf

Paul, A. M. (2004). *The cult of personality: How personality tests are leading us to miseducate our children, mismanage our companies, and misunderstand ourselves.* New York, NY: Free Press.

Phelps, M. E., Kuhl, D. E., & Mazziota, J. C. (1981). Metabolic mapping of the brain's response to visual stimulation: Studies in humans. *Science, 211*(4489), 1445–1448. doi:10.1126/science.6970412

Pichot, P. (1984). Centenary of the birth of Hermann Rorschach. *Journal of Personality Assessment, 48*(6), 591–596. doi:10.1207/s15327752jpa4806_3

Pickover, C. A. (2001). *Wonders of numbers.* New York, NY: Oxford.

Pingitore, R., Dugoni, B. L., Tindale, R. S., & Spring, B. (1994). Bias against overweight job applicants in a simulated employment interview. *Journal of Applied Psychology, 79*(6), 909–917. doi:10.1037/0021-9010.79.6.909

Piotrowski, Z. A. (1937). The Rorschach inkblot method in organic disturbances of the central nervous system. *Journal of Nervous and Mental Disease, 86,* 525–537. doi:10.1097/00005053-193711000-00002

Poston, J. M., & Hanson, W. E. (2010). Meta-analysis of psychological assessment as a therapeutic intervention. *Psychological Assessment, 22*(2), 203–212. doi:10.1037/a0018679

Ready, R. E., & Veague, H. B. (2014). Training in psychological assessment: Current practices of clinical psychology programs. *Professional Psychology: Research and Practice, 45*(4), 278–282. doi:10.1037/a0037439

Robinson, D. N. (1976). *An intellectual history of psychology.* New York, NY: MacMillan Publishing Company.

Roediger, H. L., & Karpicke, J. D. (2006). Test enhanced learning: Taking memory tests improves long-term retention. *Psychological Science, 17*(3), 249–255. doi:10.1111/j.1467-9280.2006.01693.x

Rowe, P. M. (1989). Unfavorable information and interview decisions. In R. W. Eder & G. R. Ferris (Eds.), *The employment interview: Theory, research, and practice* (pp. 77–89). Newbury Park: CA: Sage.

Russ, S. W., & Grossman-McKee, A. (1990). Affective expression in children's fantasy play, primary process thinking on the Rorschach, and divergent thinking. *Journal of Personality Assessment, 54*(3–4), 756–771. doi:10.1207/s15327752jpa5403&4_28

Sackett, P. R., & Schmitt, N. (2012). On reconciling conflicting meta-analytic findings regarding integrity test validity. *Journal of Applied Psychology, 97*(3), 550–556. doi:10.1037/a0028167

Shakespeare, W. (1606/1936). The complete works of Shakespeare (Illustrated by Rockwell Kent with a preface by Christopher Morley). Garden City: New York.

Sijtsma, K. (2009). Reliability beyond theory and into practice. *Psychometrika, 74*(1), 169–173. doi:10.1007/s11336-008-9103-y

Sijtsma, K., & Junker, B. W. (2006). Item response theory: Past performance, present developments, and future expectations. *Behaviormetrika, 33*(1), 75–102. doi:10.2333/bhmk.33.75

Slough, N., Kleinknect, R. A., & Thorndike, R. M. (1984). Relationship of the repression-sensitization scales to anxiety. *Journal of Personality Assessment, 48*(4), 378–379. doi:10.1207/s15327752jpa4804_7

Smith, C. P., Atkinson, J. W., McClelland, D. C., & Veroff, J. (1992). *Motivation and personality: Handbook of thematic content analysis* (pp. 143–152). New York, NY: Cambridge University Press. doi:10.1017/CBO9780511527937

Spangler, W. D. (1992). Validity of questionnaire and TAT measures of need for achievement: Two meta-analyses. *Psychological Bulletin, 112*(1), 140–154. doi:10.1037/0033-2909.112.1.140

Spielberger, C. D., Sydeman, S. J., & Owen, A. E. (1999). Measuring anxiety and anger with the State-Trait Anxiety Inventory (STAI) and the State-Trait Anger Expression Inventory (STAXI). In M. Maruish (Ed.), *Use of psychological testing for treatment planning and outcomes assessment* (2nd ed., pp. 993–1021). Mahwah, NJ: Lawrence Erlbaum Associates, Publishers.

Spiller, H. A., Hale, J. R., & De Boer, J. Z. (2002). The Delphic oracle: A multidisciplinary defense of the gaseous vent theory. *Clinical Toxicology, 40*(2), 189–196.

Stanton, J. M. (2001). Galton, Pearson, and the peas: A brief history of linear regression for statistics instructors. *Journal of Statistics Education, 9*(3).

Synergy (The Compost Heap) (2007, February 22). [untitled]. Downloaded from http://www.veggieboards.com/forum/17-compost-heap/62207-high-iq-2.html

Tavakol, M., & Dennick, R. (2011). Making sense of coefficient alpha. *Internaltional Journal of Medical Education, 2*, 53–55.

Teng, S. (1942—1943). Chinese influence on the western examination system. *Harvard Journal of Asiatic Studies, 7*(4), 267–312. doi:10.2307/2717830

Terman, L. M. (1922, December 27). The great conspiracy or the impulse imperious of intelligence testers, psychoanalyzed and exposed by Mr. Lippmann. *New Republic, 33*, 116–120.

Terman, L. M. (1942). The revision procedures. In Q. McNemar (Ed.), *The revision of the Stanford-Binet Scale* (pp. 1–14). New York, NY: Houghton Mifflin Company.

Thurstone, L. L. (1928). Attitudes can be measured. *American Journal of Sociology, 33*, 529–554. doi:10.1086/214483

Thurstone, L. L. (1932). *The reliability and validity of tests.* Ann Arbor, MI: Edwards Brothers.

Underwager, R., & Hollida, W. (1993). Misuse of psychological tests in forensic settings: Some horrible examples. *American Journal of Forensic Psychology, 11*, 55–75.

Watson, D., & Clark, L. A. (1997). Measurement and mismeasurement of mood: Recurrent and emergent issues. *Journal of Personality Assessment, 68*(2), 267–296. doi:10.1207/s15327752jpa6802_4

Weiner, I. B. (1994). The Rorschach Inkblot Method (RIM) is not a test: Implications for theory and practice. *Journal of Personality Assessment, 62*(3), 498–504.

Westen, D. (1991). Clinical assessment of object relations using the TAT. *Journal of Personality Assessment, 56*(1), 56–74. doi:10.1207/s15327752jpa5601_6

Wilson, T. D. (1994). The proper protocol: Validity and completeness of verbal reports. *Psychological Science, 5*(5), 249–252. doi:10.1111/j.1467-9280.1994.tb00621.x

Wilson, T. D., & Dunn, E. W. (2004). Self-knowledge: Its limits, value, and potential for improvement. *Annual Review of Psychology, 55*, 493–518. doi:10.1146/annurev.psych.55.090902.141954

Winter, D. G. (1998). "Toward a science of personality psychology": David McClelland's development of empirically derived TAT measures. *History of Psychology, 1*(2), 130–153. doi:10.1037/1093-4510.1.2.130

Wong, M. R. (1984). MMPI Scale Five: Its meaning, or lack thererof. *Journal of Personality Assessment, 48*(3), 279–284. doi:10.1207/s15327752jpa4803_9

Yoffe, E. (2014, October 7). Park the car in ___ Yard: Prudie advises a Harvard student embarrassed to say the school's name. *Slate.* Retrieved from http://www.slate.com/articles/life/dear_prudence/2014/10/dear_prudence_i_m_a_harvard_student_who_says_i_go_to_school_in_boston.html

Index

www.ingramcontent.com/pod-product-compliance
Lightning Source LLC
LaVergne TN
LVHW052310200926
848481LV00002B/519